MANAGEMENT TOOLS
IV

For Helen

CLAUDE ROSSELET
GEORG SENONER

ENACTING SOLUTIONS

Management Constellations
an innovative approach to problem-solving
and decision-making in organizations

With an introduction by Gunthard Weber

LEDIZIONI

© 2013 Edizioni Ledizioni LediPublishing
Via Alamanni 11 – 20141 Milan - Italy
http://www.ledizioni.it
e-mail: info@ledizioni.it

ENACTING SOLUTIONS

System Constellations – an innovative approach to problem-solving in business and organizations

With an introduction by Gunthard Weber

Original Title "Management Macht Sinn"
Publisher: Carl-Auer Verlag GmbH
Häusserstraße 14 – 69115 Heidelberg, Germany 2010.
Copyright ©: Claude Rosselet & Georg Senoner, 2010

English Translation by David Cotton

Italian Edition: July 2011
English Edition: March 2013

ISBN 978-88-6705-082-6 (print)
ISBN 978-88-6705-083-3 (ebook)

CONTENTS

Preface	11
Note of thanks	13
Introduction	15

PART I - ORGANIZATION CONSTELLATIONS – PUTTING THE SPOTLIGHT ON KNOWLEDGE — 19

1. SYSTEM CONSTELLATION AND COMPLEXITY — 25

1.1 To get to the bottom of the matter	25
1.2 What happens in system constellations?	26
1.2.1 The representative as a sounding board of implicit knowledge	26
1.2.2 The process of the system constellation	27
1.3 Example of a constellation	28
1.4 "Scenic protocol" for using collective intelligence	39
1.5 System constellation and learning organization management tool?	40
1.6 System constellation – a completely normal	42
1.6.1 Constellation work – a present-day oracle?	42
1.6.2 The validity of the images of a constellation	43
1.6.3 System constellation and management systems	44

2. THE MURMURING OF IMPLICIT KNOWLEDGE — 45

2.1 Implicit and explicit knowledge	46
2.2 Renunciation of the magic of the stored knowledge	47
2.3 From data to knowledge – and back again	48
2.4 Knowledge as a complex testing operation – the structuring agents of organizations	49
2.4.1 Excursus: what holds an organization together?	50
2.5 Rules and routines	54
2.6 Rules in social systems	55
2.6.1 Grammatical rules	55
2.6.2 Informal rules	56
2.6.3 Technical rules	56
2.7 System constellation as a receptor for implicit social knowledge	57

PART II - GUIDELINES FOR CONSTELLATION WORK IN MANAGEMENT CONTEXTS — 61

3. MOMENTS OF SUCCESS — 65

3.1 Observation of the terms and conditions of membership — 65
3.2 Respect of seniority and priority — 66
3.3 Recognition of greater responsibility and commitment — 67
3.4 Development of individual performances and skills — 68

4. SETTINGS OF CONSTELLATION WORK — 69

4.1 Team Setting – Management Constellations — 70
4.1.1 Constellation work in management contexts — 71
4.2 "Open" seminars — 76
4.3 Individual setting — 78
    4.3.1 Constellation work at the table — 78
    4.3.2 Constellation work in the room — 79

5. THE SEQUENCE OF THE CONSTELLATION — 81

5.1 About the role of the facilitator — 81
5.2 Framing the question — 82
5.3 Determining the elements needed for constellations — 82
5.4 Selecting and positioning the representatives — 84
5.5 Interpretation of a constellation image — 85
5.6 Interventions — 88
5.7 Conclusion — 89

6. SELECTED MENTAL MODELS AND CORRESPONDING CONSTELLATION FORMATS — 91

6.1 Management and Leadership — 92
    6.1.1 St. Gallen Management Model — 93
    6.1.2 Epidauros Model — 97
    6.1.3 Applying the Epidauros Model — 100
    6.1.4 Values and resources triangle — 101
    6.1.5 TCI Model — 105
6.2 Strategy and Innovation — 108
    6.2.1 Strategy Maps — 109

6.2.2 Butterfly model	110
6.2.3 Square of values	114
6.2.4 Development of potential	117
6.3 Problem solving and decision making	118
6.3.1 Tetralemma	118
6.3.2 Structure of a problem	120
6.3.3 Resolving conflicts	124
7. COMPLEMENTARY METHODS AND TECHNIQUES	**129**
7.1 Dialogue	129
7.2 World Café	130
7.3 Open Space	132
7.4 Dialogic Interview	133
7.5 Fish Bowl	133
7.6 The recurring question	133
7.7 Four rooms of change	134
8. CONSTELLATION WORK AS SENSEMAKING	**139**
SELECTED BIBLIOGRAPHY	**147**
THE AUTHORS	**153**

Preface

As I read the draft of this book two lines of a poem by Börries von Münchhausen came to my mind:
> *"But as the day sneaked through the gardens,*
> *the white lilac had blossomed..."*

I will follow this inspiration because I presume that this book will, for the moment at least, rarely find its way to the desks of managers who might be irritated by my inspiration. I see it mainly in the hands of business consultants and coaches. That the "white lilac" of Management Constellations really exists is still an insiders' tip among managers. It is just starting to blossom but this book reveals that this extraordinary approach is already sneaking through the gardens and it gives us a glance of what it could look like once it unfolds its brightness, effectiveness and beauty in more and more companies. As in 1975 I was asked by several colleagues: "Have you ever attended a seminar by Bert Hellinger?" – in those days he was known only to a small circle of insiders – today it could happen that when facing difficult issues in your organisation you will be asked: "Have you ever tried a management constellation?"

There are a remarkable number of things that I like in this book:

It is compact and manageable so it can be read even by busy people. The authors present the contents in a well-structured and differentiated way with clear and vivid case-studies. The reference to the theories developed by C.O. Scharmer and K.E. Weick are stimulating and the comparison with the process of management constellations shows that in other fields similar approaches to consulting and management have been developed. The main difference is the focus on the language of body and space and on other dimensions of awareness.

The book presents itself in an unpretentious manner. Sure, it wants to convince the reader of the remarkable potential of this still young approach, but it does so without missionary zeal and points in detail to the challenges both for the practitioners and for the management teams that want to use it. Thus it appears clearly that the methodology is quite demanding and requests a lot of experience and background knowledge on the side of the consultant who wants to make use of it. More so than appears at first sight.

The possibilities to gain and generate information through management constellations as well as the reciprocally stimulating transformation of images into language and vice versa are presented in detail. This is particularly helpful for generating accurate hypotheses as well as for implementing concrete strategies.

Theory and practice are well mixed, although the main focus lies on the application in management contexts. You will be pleased to find very little speculation and, instead, a lively and comprehensive description of real cases. The reader will encounter lots of pointers for reflection and for action and this book will certainly, as did the previous book, stimulate profound discussions and initiate interesting developments. This book is trendsetting and innovative for practitioners of system constellations as it shows how one can tie in with the culture and language of management when presenting this potentially disconcerting method. It also explains how system constellations can be effectively integrated with other management techniques.

The approach of Management Constellations and Organizational Constellations is still in the phase of development despite having been successfully tried and tested over the last few years. In my opinion the potential range of applications of this method have not yet been fully explored and understood. As management constellations ignite the sense of possibilities in organizations, I wish that the method itself will gradually unfold its potential. This book could contribute to it being, in my opinion, currently the best introduction not only to management constellations but to organizational constellations in general. Therefore it deserves to command widespread attention and I very much wish that it will get it.

In many gardens of this world this lilac is already blooming.

Gunthard Weber
Wiesloch, July 2010

Note of thanks

To begin with our thanks go to Gunthard Weber as one the major promoters of the organizational constellation. He is our very dear friend and mentor and has supported our work on many occasions. We also thank our clients very sincerely. They have engaged in an unusual experiment from which we have learned a lot. We developed management constellations in discussions and workshops with Henriette K. Lingg and put them to the test in practice. Our findings are also based on the knowledge of many teachers and colleagues. They include Guni Leila Baxa, Michael Blumenstein, Christine Essen, Siegfried Essen, Stefan Hausner, Albrecht Mahr, Peter Müller Egloff, Bernd Schmid, Gunther Schmidt, Sneh Viktoria Schnabel, Jakob and Sieglinde Schneider, Fritz Simon, Kuno Sohm, Gerhard Stey, Jan Jakob and Bibi Stam, Insa Sparrer and Matthias Varga von Kibéd. The latter two developed a grammar in the course of the 1990s that benefitted the formation of a theory. We have consciously and unconsciously integrated some of this in our practice and book. At this point, we should also especially like to thank Regula Heller Rosselet and Markus Pohlmann for their critical revision of our manuscript and the ideas for improvements in content and style that originate from them.

Claude Rosselet & Georg Senoner

Männedorf and Bolzano, January 2010

Introduction

Gunthard Weber's 1993 book "Zweierlei Glück" (*Love's Hidden Symmetry*) and the subsequent workshops add a strong momentum to the procedure of family constellations developed by Bert Hellinger. Systemic-constellation work spread quickly throughout the German-speaking world and beyond, especially in Latin America, Eastern Europe, Russia and Asia.

In 1994, the management consultants Thomas Siefer and Michael Wingenfeld invited Bert Hellinger to a seminar dealing with how constellation work could be applied to organizations. That was the beginning of the "organization constellation". Until today this branch of constellation work has been denied its great breakthrough; in spite of the intensive efforts of the precursors of this method, especially of Gunthard Weber, to make this procedure known world-wide.

There are however niches where managers enthuse about this procedure and integrate it into their repertoire of management tools. A stable bond of trust in a consultant, who only applies constellation work if it is practical, is a pre-condition. Usually the method is linked with other intervention practices.

This book is aimed at managers and consultants, who want to use system constellations and who consciously want to break new ground by "developing the future" (Mandl 2006, p. 267 ff) whether it is because they want to develop the potential of "their" organization in a more innovative way or because they have understood that approaches based purely on reason often lack mobilizing power.

Managers and consultants consistently note that much of what has been planned is not implemented and that on the other hand other things that were not planned successfully emerge. Obviously the interface between planning and implementation is beyond a purely rational management. This is especially noticeable in the case of radical changes. Basic innovations are very rarely stimulated by a business plan.

The driving forces for innovation are for the main part hidden in the tacit knowledge of organizations.

Rationalistic approaches to decision making have something in common: they tend to trivialise and take too short a view of circumstances. In doing so the following success factors are undervalued or systematically suppressed: wishes and longings, as well as intuition hardened by practical experience.

Excellence is based precisely on these elements. However excellence is also consistently overlooked because it is not strident or showy, but exercises discipline and leads a quiet existence.

It is a necessary pre-condition for renewal is to see the current situation as it is very comprehensively and lucidly. This avoids reaching a premature judgement. If this is examined with due care and attention, then those driving forces come to the fore. As a result, things can be easier to shape so that they can be used to devise the next consistent move into the future. Just that seems to us to be the secret of emergence, namely a future that conforms to its origins.

Nevertheless planning is by no means unnecessary. One of the main tasks of management is to equip all projects with the necessary resources, however limited. A rational approach is very much called for here. Planning, however, only makes sense if it creates a vivid picture of the future. Otherwise the past is simply carried forward to the future.

As mentioned at the beginning, constellation work has not yet gained wider access to the upper echelons of the company's management. Presumably there are a few obstacles that cannot be brushed aside so easily. If we mention this here, it does not mean that we want to dishearten our readers from the beginning. Quite to the contrary: only by knowing the obstacles can consultants and managers, who are enthusiastic about constellation work, use their strategies to implement the methods effectively. What then do we need to pay attention to?

- It seems rather threatening to some managers that the conditions and the dynamics in organizations can be revealed with the help of the system constellation. Occasionally it is easier to live with ambiguity than with clarity.

- Focussing on body awareness and feelings breaks with the usual communication behavior and can lead to embarrassment.

- Whenever very risky decisions have to be taken, managers prefer to rely on (the myth of) scientifically safe "tools".

- The procedure of a constellation is regarded as being too time-consuming for many managers, because it requires special settings and a facilitator, who introduces and applies the method competently. Constellation work cannot be applied as easily as traditional brain storming for example.

- It appears to us however that the greatest obstacle is that many managers, but also consultants, who rely exclusively on rational methods, do not really trust constellation work. Consequently it is dismissed as a mind game, as something esoteric, theatre, etc.

Calmly handling the objections is a promising way of breaking the ice at the right moment by advancing the invitation "Let us just try an experiment for once!" instead of preaching enthusiastically for a "wonderful method".

In **part I** of this book we explain how complexity can be visualized with the help of the system constellation and we demonstrate this by means of a detailed example. We also sketch the methodological background. As we demonstrate, the system constellation can very well be linked with the more recent concepts of the "learning organization". Then we discuss concepts such as "implicit knowledge" and "social intelligence". We also illustrate in detail the relationship between the practices of social systems and the rules on which they are based. The system constellation can shed light on the implicit orders of organizations. This is very useful for the management of the rules, the crucial point of change management. It opens up new possibilities to managers and consultants for intervening in social systems.

In **part II** we turn completely to the method of the system constellation and its application in management contexts.

PART I

ORGANIZATION CONSTELLATIONS

PUTTING THE SPOTLIGHT ON KNOWLEDGE

We begin with three stories from the everyday management scene.

They all have something in common:
• A management team feels itself challenged by a question it cannot answer.
• The traditional methods of problem solving and decision making do not produce a result that makes sense.
• Somehow the discussions go round in circles with argument and counter-argument cancelling each other out.
• Gradually this escalates into bad-temper.

Ignoring healthy common sense

A leisure park with an extended complex of pools, several shopping centres and a hotel complex is in real need of a renovation. The location was once the showpiece for a large retail chain. The company management decided therefore on a comprehensive redevelopment. By doing this, the hotel complex should also become more attractive, because the below average occupancy rate gave cause for dissatisfaction.

Several areas of the business were involved in the plan. A relaunch of the whole location was meant to be carried out on the basis of a marketing concept. The objective was to create links with earlier glorious times. However, things could not really get started properly. The marketing concept remained a fragment. On the other hand, individual parts of the plan were implemented speedily. The business management decided therefore to merge all activities into one comprehensive project that was to speed up the whole thing. However, the opposite happened. The relaunch took on enormous dimensions on paper. Suddenly, there were differences of opinion??? about the organizational integration of the complex. Wearily the project leader threw in the towel. Management thought that they were facing ruin.

Then something happened that nobody had thought possible.

The project team was disbanded. The differences could be rectified in no time at all. The members of the management team agreed on an action plan and made it their top priority. The chief financial officer (CFO) was extremely satisfied. Prior to this he had been blamed for the disastrous situation, but in the end he was thanked for his exceptional dedication to the project.

Failure to communicate

A business unit of a large manufacturer had lost an important customer due to deficient product quality. Subsequently, the quality could be improved with considerable development effort. It even overtook that of its competitor who had stepped into the breach. However, the lost customer could not be won back. The management team was at a loss and had in its own words "already tried everything" and now wanted to find out what it had failed to do in its extensive activities.

Then something happened that nobody had thought possible.

The manufacturer specifically sent an expert with strong communication skills to the customer he was wooing. The expert agreed precise needs regarding the quality of the products with his colleagues and other specialists there. After a year, the manufacturer succeeded in winning back "his" client. As a result, the teamwork on developing products together with the client was boosted. Today, this manufacturer is the key supplier of this client. The element "communication" of the marketing mix is now the business unit's strongest point. Experts focus not only on their own products. They discuss their wishes with their customer's experts.

Lost hope

The Italian subsidiary of a German company and its parent company had been taken over by a Japanese company. The self-confident business leader together with his management team subsequently considered how the Italian subsidiary could play a supporting role in the new structure. He clearly felt the doubts of his managers. What should be done to prevent the Japanese from switching the production of a relatively standardised product to a low-wage country and closing its plant in Italy? The misgivings and fears of the managers were based especially on preconceptions and not on the precise programmes of the Japanese. This was nor a good basis for developing strategies for the future.

However, something happened then that nobody had thought possible.

The managers decided to collaborate with the German parent company on production. Such a thing would not have been imaginable in the past! A further move consisted of uncoupling the Italian channels of distribution from the Italian production and bringing it closer to the remaining channels of distribution of the group of companies. Until now Italian sales had mainly concentrated on marketing the products manufactured in Italy. The changes fitted in excellently to the pan-European sales concept that the Japanese approved a little later. The Italians were already well prepared for this and collaborated constructively in implementing it without the otherwise usual reservations.

We have suppressed an element in all three stories and for this reason have possibly strained the patience of our readers. What was so decisive that it brought about a surprising new solution?

First of all the managers had understood that the problem could only be solved if all parties concerned jointly took part in searching for a solution. They decided not to pass the elusive hot potato around. Lonely night-time brooding and quiet manoeuvring behind the backs of colleagues gave way to discussions together about how to succeed.

Even the managers were convinced that no additional resources needed to be put into analyses, expert reports and plans. After all there was sufficient experience in the team in order to reach plausible and meaningful solutions for all participants. Furthermore, the solutions on paper appeared if anything to have diverted from what was essential.

The managers therefore decided on a plan of action with which they could bring the "collective intelligence" of their whole team into play.

It had become clear to them that when dealing with the future it is often not helpful to rely solely on rationalist approaches. As the latest research in neurobiology documents, wishes, longings, intuition and experience tempered by practice play the central role regarding decisions on the future. But all these success factors transmit only weak signals; often enough downgraded by people who think they know better.

But which instruments are sensitive enough also to detect hidden, so-called implicit knowledge? And which of them are at the same time intelligent enough to interpret the information gleaned in such way that the information emerging from this offers guidelines for future action?

With system constellations presented in the next chapter and subsequently discussed in detail, management has come by a method that can assess risks in confusing situations and create clear guidance for decisions, i.e., certainty. We impressively demonstrate this in very practical terms in section 1.3 by means of our above example of the Italian subsidiary.

CHAPTER 1

SYSTEM CONSTELLATION AND COMPLEXITY

The system constellation is a scenic representation: precise events are displayed in space and time. A kind of "moving" picture emerges and from this, conclusions are drawn that are inherent in a specific incident.

The wish to stage complicated or complex conditions and relationships is long-established. Scenic representations therefore form the cornerstones of almost all cultures. They prove that it has fascinated man since earliest times to condense and portray the essence of occurrences in a space-time sequence, that is, to put it on the scene.

The scenic representation makes something possible that no report can. It conveys what is essential in a situation in a lively sequence of pictures. However, it also renders more than a single picture because it points from the origins to the future and therefore expresses a direction of motion i.e. an intention.

1.1 To get to the bottom of the matter

In addition to explicit knowledge implicit knowledge is needed in order to comprehend situations in their inherent complexity. By this we understand knowledge that is indeed available, but without further ado is not accessible for conscious reflection. Therefore it is not very easy for us to grasp implicit knowledge. Nevertheless, a large part of expertise and excellence belongs to this dimension of knowledge: the resourcefulness of the research team, the manager's intuition, the accuracy of the precision engineer, the speed of the woman runner, the intuition of the therapist, the company's power of innovation, etc.

Figuratively speaking, explicit knowledge is comparable to that part of the iceberg that presents itself above the water level to the eye of the beholder. The much larger part however cannot be seen and we can only guess how big the iceberg may be and what tensions lie dormant in it. The traditional economic information systems fall short precisely in the case of implicit knowledge. They focus almost exclusively on explicit knowledge.

Therefore they only represent a small part of what makes up a situation in all its aspects.

In many cases, however, it is necessary to get a picture of the whole. The system constellation is ideal for this. It is effective, quick, and unconventional and can gather information on the circumstances of the case that are otherwise not immediately accessible. The procedure makes it possible to include all parts of knowledge in the calculation when making decisions in situations that bear a high risk.

The resource and solution orientated approach that includes collective intelligence also facilitates the cohesion of the team. This is especially important in the case of controversial decisions where complete mutual trust is requested. Decisions are then backed even if they are difficult to implement.

1.2 What happens in system constellations?

In system constellations, aspects of a complex situation are presented in the room with the help of representatives – a kind of role-player. In the process it amounts to a twin clarification. On the one hand, the situation is visualized – put in the spotlight – and on the other hand a gradual succession of solution options can be elaborated. In this chapter we give an overview of how information can be gained with this unusual method when complex decisions have to be met. In section 1.3, we illustrate with the help of an example how participants could find the answer to a difficult question with the help of a constellation.

1.2.1 The representative as a sounding board of implicit knowledge

In contrast to role-playing – which is familiar to many in work contexts – the representatives are not given any instructions in the case of system constellation, because the stage directions would express first and foremost explicit knowledge. The representatives obtain their directions as it were through the "representative perception" emerging in the "field" (Varga von Kibéd u. Sparrer 2000, p. 98). They quite literally become sounding boards for implicit knowledge.

Their body perceptions deliver the data from which information about a situation is gathered. As distinct from the sociogram, it does not concentrate on a static image but on a sequence of images that show the way to the solution.

The constellation creates a kind of communicative space, or a "field of knowledge", as Albrecht Mahr puts it, that provides representatives with immediate access to the deeper-lying layers of a "challenged" situation via the specific place in a relational structure.

To date there has been no consistent theory for this aspect of the dynamic diagnostic tool "system constellation". The representatives' perceptions, often so impressively noticeable, are still awaiting a scientific explanation. The theory of language games of the philosopher Ludwig Wittgenstein (Sparrer 2006, p. 81 ff) gives some clues of how the "basic Grammar" in constellations functions. According to it language "portrays" structures of reality adequately. Other attempts to explain this fall back on the concept of the "morphic resonance" described by the biochemist Rupert Sheldrake in his theory of the morphogenetic field (Sheldrake 1981). More recent attempts at explanations draw on quantum physics (Schneider 2007, p. 18 ff). The findings of neurobiology also explain the phenomenon of information transfer from system to system. It can be deduced from all these theories that collective intelligence is "embedded" in the relationships between the members of a social system – or in the *field* of relationships – and not in the members themselves. The members just express the quality of relationships.

1.2.2 The process of the system constellation

System constellations therefore provide descriptions based on experience of causal relationships in live systems, for example in organizations. They use the language of the body and space to find solutions to complex decision making problems. Aspects of a situation are presented in the room with the help of representatives. In other words a constellation is set up.

As a rule, the following is observed: someone or a complete team with a precise concern, such as an unsolved problem or difficult question, chooses representatives from workshop participants for the relevant aspects of a problem. According to the subject these aspects can be either individuals or groups involved in the situation. They can however also be abstract elements like the mutually exclusive options of a dilemma, or the objectives and obstacles in a blocked situation. Likewise, a representative often identified as the "focus" is chosen for the individual or group from whose point of view the problem is perceived. Subsequently, this person positions the representatives in the room by following his or her intuition or inner image (Weber 1995, p. 181 ff).

In the following phase of the constellation, the facilitator asks the representatives in turn about their body perceptions. The dynamics, underlying a problematic situation, can be developed from the representatives' perceptions". The dysfunctional patterns that impede development can be detected. Options of solutions disclose themselves by re-positioning the representatives and checking their reactions. Even the smallest re-positioning of a representative can produce differences in the body perceptions of the other representatives and allow for a further move of one or several representatives.

In the course of the constellation, it is essential to develop a line-up in which the representatives hold together in a harmonious relationship. This is recorded by them physically for example as "relief", "relaxation" or "release". Such a process usually lasts for about half an hour. It can also be shorter or – in difficult situations – much longer. Gradually, surprising points of view emerge about how a specific matter could be followed up, precisely because the procedure includes the non-verbal and emotional sides of an issue.

Such a way of clarifying a problem and identifying a solution requires a specific setting. Firstly, it needs a circle of people who are ready to engage again and again in the experiment of the "representative perception" and to vouch for the problematic aspects of a situation. Secondly, people are needed who are flexible enough "to experience" answers to their unexplained questions in an unusual form. Thirdly, a facilitator is essential to hold the overall setting, to help clarify the question, and to support the process of identifying the solution with his questions and interventions.

1.3 Example of a constellation

In order to illustrate a precise constellation, we fall back on our story "Lost Hope" from the introductory text of part I. As a reminder: the Italian branch of a German company and its parent company had been taken over by a Japanese group of companies and the manager commissioned a consultant to accompany him and his management team in this critical phase of post-merger-integration. The manager had formulated his objective for the consultants as follows: he wanted to develop a strategy with his managers that assured the survival of the Italian subsidiary in the new structure and for it to remain indispensable in the future.

The managers' doubts about this objective were clearly expressed at the opening of the first workshop with the management team. The consultant contemplated how he could best divert the managers' attention away from their speculations towards the actual situation of the company. It was important to him that the managers recognized the opportunities and challenges that the new structure of ownership brought with it. As an initial step, he wanted to develop a realistic picture of the new situation based on the actual available information. This should assist the development of clear ideas for possible actions. And these could then form the basis for a new strategy. The system constellation seemed to the consultant to be the most efficient method for this purpose.

After he had explained in a few words how the system constellation works, he introduced the intervention with the following analogy:

"Please imagine the context in which you are operating is a playing field on which your company, together with other team-mates and opponents, is playing a game of survival and economic success. Since the Japanese group of companies took over, the playing field, the players and partly even the rules of the game have changed. Who are now the most important players with whom you have to collaborate or compete?"

The consultant identified, together with the management team the following important players:
- the management team of the Italian subsidiary,
- the Italian production,
- the Italian sales organization,
- the German production,
- the other sales organizations,
- the European headquarters of the group of companies,
- the Japanese group of companies,
- the customers.

After this the consultant asked the managers to imagine how the players could perhaps be placed on the playing field: "Just as with football, it is also decisive in industry for the course of the game how the team is positioned on the field."

In the next move it was a matter of setting up a picture of the situation in the room. This first image was bound to offer valuable clues through its specific constellation i.e., how the representatives relate to each other. "Even though this experiment might perhaps seem a little strange to you at first," the consultant interjected. "Simply get involved and look at what comes out. To begin with please choose two people, who together will assign their places to the representatives for their selected roles and thus produce an image of the situation. It is not really important who you choose, provided the person selected agrees and wants to take part in the experiment".

The special course of action to set up an initial constellation by two people has the following advantages:

> • Two personal perceptions, possibly not completely congruent, leave their mark on the represented image.

> • Colleagues are less likely to object that the image only reflects the view of one single member of the team.

The consultant went on to explain to the group of workshop participants: "Colleagues, whoever has been chosen as representatives, should simply pay attention to what has changed for them when they are positioned and when other representatives are gradually added. Whenever your two colleagues lead you to a position on the imaginary playing field, you will in fact experience that your body perception, feelings and thoughts change. You will also possibly perceive very precise body impulses. Please simply record it."

After the representatives had been chosen, the consultant guided the constellation as follows. He asked both appointed managers to place themselves behind the representative of the management team and lead him to a position in the room that they both felt was "right": "They arrange themselves best together without communicating by word of mouth until they agree on a position. Do not think too much or deeply about things, but let your feet and intuition guide you. You will notice when you have reached the right position. Distance, angle of vision and place in the room correspond to the relationship between the players. Simply try things out, put your trust in your intuition that will know exactly when things are right."

Both managers positioned the representatives in the room with impressive care and resolution. Step by step the picture of the situation was built up, the atmosphere in the room changed, it became completely quiet and the tension increased.

After the last representative had been positioned in the room, the consultant asked the managers who had placed the representatives: "Do you still want to change something? Please take your time and check whether the image corresponds to the situation in which you think your company now is. Both managers made minor changes to the position of a representative and then thought: "Yes, this could be right now." (Fig. 1)

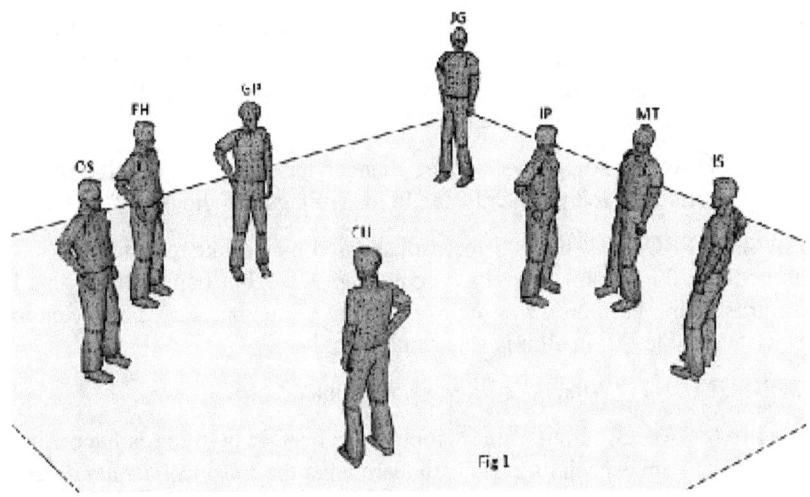

Fig. 1: Post-Merger-Integration – initial image

MT Management team (Focus)
OS other sales organizations
IP Italian production
EH European headquarters
IS Italian sales organizations
JG Japanese group
GP German production
CU customers

The consultant allowed the image to have an impact on him and a few remarkable positions occurred to him spontaneously:
- *Italian production*, the *management team* and *Italian sales* formed an isolated group on the edge of the field.
- *German* and *Italian production*s were gazing in different directions.
- The *European headquarters* had no eye contact with the representatives of both production sites.

After these first observations, he started to question the representatives individually:

CONSULTANT: "We would like to hear what you think about your position. I am going to ask you questions in the order in which you were put in position. What has changed for the *management team of the Italian subsidiary* in the course of the constellation and how has your relationship with the other elements changed?"

MANAGEMENT TEAM: "It became more oppressive as more elements were added. I feel myself to be isolated and especially under pressure from the *Italian production*. The *Japanese* are so far away that I can only see them whenever I turn round. There are so many people before me that I do not know who I should concentrate on."

CONSULTANT: "And what kind of changes has the representative of the *Italian production* felt physically and in his feelings and thoughts?"

ITALIAN PRODUCTION: "I feel isolated and would like to turn away ... I am looking for support from the *management team*, but I am not sure that I can trust them. I see our *sales division* in front of me, but it does not seem to be very reliable. All in all it is very unpleasant here."

CONSULTANT: "What does *Italian sales* think?

ITALIAN SALES: "I am at the wrong place here, everything is happening over there. I am especially curious to learn what the *European headquarters* are planning."

CONSULTANT: "What has changed for the *German production*?"

GERMAN PRODUCTION: "I am unsure and isolated. Our *customers* are far away and have no contact with me."

CONSULTANT: "What is happening with the *other sales organizations*?"

OTHER SALES ORGANIZATIONS: "Disoriented. I mostly feel the influence of the *headquarters*, but I am also wondering what the *production* and those in *Japan* want? I am mainly waiting to see what happens."

CONSULTANT: "And how does the *European headquarters* feel about things?"

EUROPEAN HEADQUARTERS: "I still have to get a grip on everything. My main focus of attention is concentrated on our *customers*. The *production sites* are too far away for me. It is stressful, but I feel strong and resolute, but also very tense."

CONSULTANT: "Yes, and what is the view from *Japan*?"

JAPANESE GROUP: "I really feel far away, calm and very attentive. I can see the *European headquarters*. The rest seems rather blurred to me."

CONSULTANT: "How will the *customers* react?"

CUSTOMERS: "All of this does not really affect me. I am mostly interested in the *European headquarters.*"

The consultant now spoke to the CEO and the managers who had been outside observers and not part of the constellation: "Whenever you listen to and watch this, do you have the impression that this corresponds more or less to reality, or are we watching the wrong movie?" They appeared impressed at how closely the image and the statements of the representatives agreed in many aspects with their own perception of the situation.

The consultant now made further enquiries about what information and pointers for possible action they could already gather from this first image.

"In any event, the *management team* has to find a position that allows it to have better contact with the *headquarters* and *customers*," was the opinion of one of the managers. "*Sales* have already said that they want to change their position."

Another manager commented: "*Our sales* have to collaborate more closely with *other sales organizations*. It is clear that *production* has the largest problem and at the moment I cannot see any solution for it."

The consultant assimilated these comments and linked them to the statements of the representatives, and, together with his own impressions, formulated a first hypothesis. The *management team* acts as if jammed between the *Italian production* and *Italian sales* and cut off from the *European headquarters*. It is very difficult to manage from such a position.

Supported by these thoughts he now made his first intervention: "We want to find out then what happens if we change a few positions. Let's begin with the *management team*. Do you feel you want to move elsewhere?"

The representative thought about this and pondered. This stressed him very much. After a while he said: "I feel as if I were paralysed."

"Then I'll try and see if we can find a better position for you," the consultant said and lightly tapped the representative on his shoulder. He led him to a position between the *European headquarters* and *Italian production* (fig. 2). Then he asked: "Is it better here, worse, the same or simply different?"

The answer was: "Definitely better, freer, clearer and above all I can see my customers." The representative was clearly more relaxed.

The consultant then turned to the other representatives and asked: "For whom does this make a difference?"

The *Italian production* reported immediately: "If anything I feel worse!"

Fig. 2: Post-Merger-Integration – intermediate result

MT Management team (Focus)
OS other sales organizations
IP Italian production
EH European headquarters

IS Italian sales organization
JG Japanese group
GP German production
CU customers

The consultant himself had various options for a change of the constellation, but he wanted to fully involve the implicit knowledge – collective intelligence – of the representatives. He went to the representative of the *Italian production* and said to him: "Look then please for a better position. Simply try out several possibilities." The representative moved around rather hesitantly at first and then said: "I am attracted towards *German production*. That is rather strange because until now they were always our arch-enemies, our real competitors!"

However, the representative of the *German production* turned spontaneously to the *Italian production* and said: "It is exactly the same for me. I am indeed still sceptical, but it is definitely better this way."

In quite a similar way, a new constellation developed into a kind of "co-creation" that all participants found definitely better and more energetic. This was partly because the consultant assigned a new position to the representatives, partly because he instructed them to follow their impulses in their search for a better position.

The time had arrived for a first "interim result". The consultant asked the representatives what they felt about this new constellation.

The *Italian sales organization* said: "I knew immediately that my place is here close to the *other sales organizations*, but I did not think that it would be so difficult to dissociate myself from *Italian production*. It only succeeded once the *management team* had moved away and *German production* had moved closer."

"It is much better and more relaxed," the *European headquarters* declared. The representatives for the production sites are still a little too far away for me."

"I feel myself torn between two conflicting options," said the *management team*. "On the one hand, I should be closer to the *European headquarters*, on the other however the *Italian production* needs me."

The expression "to be torn between two options" made the consultant prick up his ears. He interpreted it as a sign that there are two conflicting aspects in the role of the *management team*.

Such diametrically opposed tendencies always have to be dealt with in the course of a constellation. Possibly, they are an indication of logjams. With the help of a specific intervention the doubts are overcome.

"I would like to try out a test," the consultant said, turning to one of the managers in the group. "Perhaps the *management team* has two or more diverging tasks that cannot be so easily reconciled. Therefore I am selecting a new representative for *another part of the management team* and placing him near the *management team* that feels itself torn between a series of alternatives."

"Does this change anything?" the consultant asked after he had placed a representative at the side of the *management team*.

The representative of the *management team* felt strengthened and at the same time positively relieved. The *other part of the management team* felt an impulse to turn itself more towards the *Italian production*.

"So that I can now move closer to the *European headquarters*," said the representative of the *management team*. The *European headquarters* agreed very much with this: "It is much better like this!" (Fig. 3)

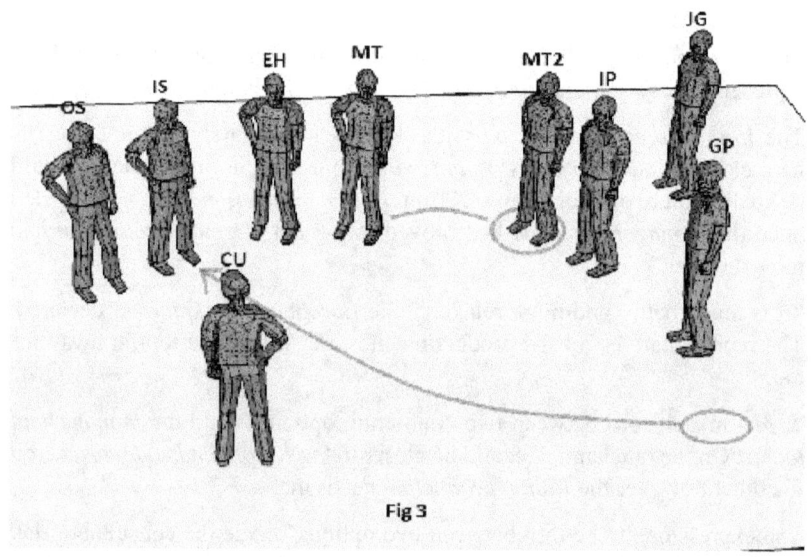

Fig. 3: Post-Merger-Integration – final image management team (Focus)

MT   Management team (Focus)
MT2 "the other part" of the management team
OS   other sales organizations
IP   Italian production
EH   European headquarters
IS   Italian sales organization
JG   Japanese group
DP   German production
CU   customers

The consultant now had the impression that the current constellation was in harmony. In addition, the many changes brought a whole lot of information to light. However, he still wanted to ask the representatives, with whom he had not worked directly, one last time about their perceptions.

The *customers* considered: "We are very happy now. Everything is concentrated on us."

The *Japanese group* declared: "If things continue to develop so well, I'll have no reason to interfere. I have not moved. I am happy here."

With this the consultant closed the constellation: "Many thanks! Please now leave your respective roles very consciously. We'll have a short pause and then within the framework of a joint discussion clarify what you have learned from this exercise and how it can be applied."

In the first round of the following dialogue each manager described in turn what had impressed him most about the constellation. Afterwards the participants prepared the first precise moves together.

No doubt the most important insight is that the closing of ranks (in the literal sense of the word) between the German and Italian production sites presented a possible and sensible solution. For the managers of this company such a move is a real "revolution". Until now they had always regarded the production plant of the German parent company as their real business rivals who snapped up the products with the most lucrative margins, but left the most difficult projects to the Italians. As a reaction they concealed all innovations from the "Germans" for as long as possible in order not to surrender their own competitive advantage. The idea of cooperation was so remote to the managers that it would indeed hardly ever come up in a normal discussion as it would have been shaped too much by the traditional prejudices.

The constellation process had impressed the managers and they held the solutions that became apparent in the course of the constellation as very sensible. The CEO and the production manager decided immediately afterwards to fly to the parent company in the Ruhr area in order to submit a suggestion for cooperation.

The result of this approach was a plan to set up a joint production plant in Poland in the same year where the production of cost-critical products would be outsourced.

A further important pointer that had been seen in the constellation was the detachment of the Italian sales system from the Italian production and its convergence with the other sales systems of the group. Italian sales had hitherto concentrated mainly on marketing the products manufactured in their own plants in Italy. The new positioning that came to light during the constellation pointed the way to a closer cooperation with the sales systems of other countries. In the long run, this should benefit all partners involved because in this way the complete range of products could be offered Europe-wide with full commitment.

The reorganization of sales was one of the first measures the Japanese headquarters would take a few months later. At that time, the Italians were already well prepared for this and collaborated constructively in the new structure without their usual resistance.

The managers also accepted the splitting up of the management team into two subgroups as an important hint. One could dedicate itself to the European headquarters and the other to Italian production. They discussed how they could boost their presence in the headquarters in order to represent Italian interests effectively and at the same time not neglect the management of the Italian branch. The CEO had hitherto been heavily involved in running the day-to-day business. As a result of the new organization his duties were re-packaged and some of them delegated to members of the management team.

In the end, the statement of the representative of the Japanese group that he would indeed monitor developments very closely, but nevertheless from a distance reduced fears of an immediate closure of the Italian production. The managers took courage and were able to develop their vision of the future within the framework of the following strategy workshops and decide the appropriate strategic measures to take.

This therefore was the prelude to a very successful post-merger integration. The system constellation had produced a completely surprising, radical change of opinion. The managers had overcome the paralysis that had befallen them from their speculations on the consequences of the takeover. They had sounded out their scope for action in the constellation and subsequently used these adroitly. They succeeded in finding a good position in the group's global organization.

After less than two years the management of the total European production was assigned to the CEO of the Italian branch. He proudly reported that the Italian branch was now delivering special products from its own plant to the Far East.

Summary

We sum up again the most important moves of the constellation so that you understand the course of events better.

The starting point for this was a clearly defined request from the customer we had advised. In the case described the consultant's objective was to create good conditions in order subsequently to be able to develop a strategy that secured the survival of the Italian company as previously agreed with the CEO.

The consultant pursued a systemic approach and focussed his attention on the relevant context factors and the interdependencies between the participating players. He therefore invited the managers to widen their horizons and reconsider their situation from a very different point of view.

The consultant faced the problem by adopting a solution-oriented attitude. He assumed that his customer had the necessary resources in order to find an adequate solution. It was self-evident for him that the rudiments for a solution were already lying dormant in the team's implicit knowledge. Only a few skilled interventions were needed to rouse it. Therefore he asked the representatives time and again during the constellation to pursue their instincts and try out new positions.

In order to manage the tricky problems that arose from the merger, the consultant chose a system level that helped to highlight the relevant dynamics. As an introduction to this first sequence he used the metaphor of a game of football. From the outset, the players have to position themselves strategically and skillfully on the playing field before they can succeed with their tactical moves.

The constellation form and its corresponding elements were derived according to the selected system level. The consultant decided on an organization constellation with the management team as the focus. He based the constellation on the *point of view of the management team* and had functional units of the company and its circumstances – and not individuals –set up.

The scenic work was the main part of the intervention. The constellation allowed managers to experiment with important aspects of their new situation. A precise future situation was anticipated using the collective intelligence of the team. As David Bohm has already shown, collective thinking is more powerful than individual thinking (Bohm 2002).

The translation from the analogue language of the scene into the logically sequential language of everyday was last but not least. This took place partly during the constellation, but especially in the subsequent dialogue. The participants took up relevant scenic moments and described them in their daily language so that they could be used for further decision making.

1.4 "Scenic protocol" for using collective intelligence

In recent years, several settings for using "collective intelligence" have found their way into the processes of organizations' strategic decision making. Open Space (Harrison Owen), World Café (Juanita Brown) and Dialog (David Bohm) are already very widespread.

The system constellation ties up with these methods which use collective intelligence. On the one hand, it avails itself – at least in its original form – of a collective of actors who effectively step into the roles representing a specific situation, but it also creates a "social" space for communication in which very specific knowledge comes into play: *the knowledge that comes with experience.* Bearing social systems in mind, knowledge is to be understood, as a kind of "latent" social semantic structure, "which emerges from the relationships", as Dirk Baecker puts it (Baecker 1999, p. 78). A special characteristic of this knowledge is that it cannot be put in language.

The system constellation clarifies situations not only at a linguistic level. It makes social events immediately physically perceptible and imparts the emotional qualities through perception. The system constellation therefore makes a new form of code available. Its special feature is its physically affective dimension. This is activated by people stepping into the picture for a short time and becoming part of this picture. Our familiar subject-object separation is suspended for a few moments. People embody their positions, as it were.

The system constellation is similar in parts to Ralf Bohnsack's method of objective hermeneutics and the narrative interview described as "procedure of reconstructive social research". These procedures aim at finding out the genuine "social" elements, i.e., those not developed by the individual. These and especially the narrative interview are based on the basic assumption of a "homology of narrative and experience" (Heinz Bude). What is meant by this is that a narrator re-tells the story as he has experienced it, i.e., he reproduces his experience "in what is relevant and focuses on constituting his identity and consequently also on what is relevant for action for him" (Bohnsack 1999, p. 57). Something very similar happens in constellation work. The world of experience of a client system finds its very specific embodiment in the arrangement of the representatives that changes from scene to scene.

Seen this way the system constellation can be described as a scenic record of a specific event. In a co-creative communications process between representatives and the facilitator a functional solution is gradually developed for a precise problem. With this process the "driving forces" that characterize a specific situation are elaborated.

1.5 System constellation and learning organization

The system constellation can be integrated very well with methods developed under the concept of the "learning organization" which fall back preferentially on self' reflexive processes. System constellations enable consciousness to become self-consciousness. For example, Claus Otto Scharmer's Theory U, a systematic method for discovering the future of an organization, is ideal for constellation work (Scharmer 2000): "In order to be able to operate successfully in a newly emerging business situation, managers must be proficient in the skill of sensing what the future holds and implementing and embodying it. "That sounds as if Scharmer wants to allude to the system constellation that, however, he does not mention. Indeed, in the 3rd and 4th dimension of Scharmer's transformation process – at the level of "imagination" and "primary knowing" or "presencing" – precisely that knowledge of experience becomes accessible that is the basis for any kind of development in a company (graph. 1).

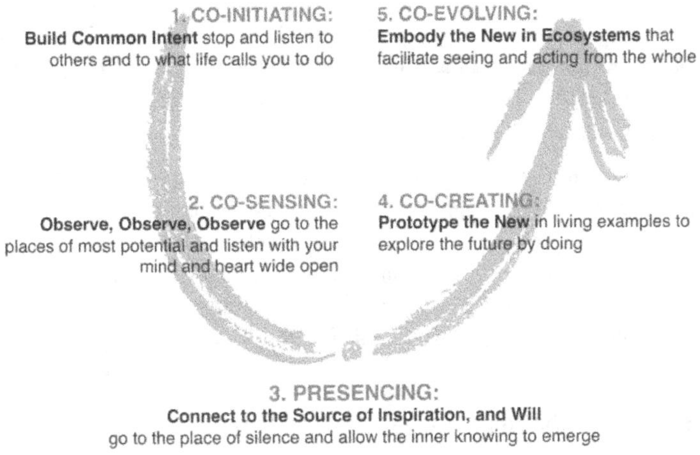

1. CO-INITIATING:
Build Common Intent stop and listen to others and to what life calls you to do

5. CO-EVOLVING:
Embody the New in Ecosystems that facilitate seeing and acting from the whole

2. CO-SENSING:
Observe, Observe, Observe go to the places of most potential and listen with your mind and heart wide open

4. CO-CREATING:
Prototype the New in living examples to explore the future by doing

3. PRESENCING:
Connect to the Source of Inspiration, and Will
go to the place of silence and allow the inner knowing to emerge

Graph. 1: Claus Otto Scharmer's U-process (2009)

Until today there are only few, and partly time-consuming methods for developing this knowledge. Here then the system constellation is exactly the right solution. It is easy but not simple.

Under the title Leading from the future Claus Otto Scharmer explores how hidden structures of social entities can be made systematically accessible. In the process, the idea occurs to him that there has to be a kind of Archimedes point as the lynchpin for offsetting the structure of a social field (Scharmer 2005). He locates this point more precisely inside an observing system – be it an individual manager, a team or a company in its "field structures of attention". Scharmer distinguishes between 4 different modes of attention and with it 4 closely connected categories of intentions. You can move backwards and forwards between these 4 levels, however, the result is completely different in each dimension. Scharmer describes this as follows:

If I am listening from level 1, the discussion is frozen in old-established models of the past (downloading).

If I am listening from level 2, I discuss with the other person (reflecting).

If I am listening from level 3, I conjure up a dialogue in which I experience direct contact, association and unity with the other person and which breaks down the dividing boundary between me and the other person (imagining).

If I am listening from level 4, I begin to participate in the formation of a new inner space through which a peaceful, creative presence begins to appear and a direct response to my highest future potential begins to become tangible and productive in real terms (presencing).

The search for innovative ways of coping with the future asks individuals, teams and organizations to get involved increasingly on the 3rd and 4th levels when identifying a problem. At the same time Scharmer is completely aware that his way "inwards" might be unfamiliar to many. He also refers to the three most important obstacles that have to be overcome: the voice of judgement, the voice of cynicism and the voice of fear.

1.6 System constellation – a completely normal management tool?

The fact that the system constellation allows insights into hitherto hidden aspects of events could tempt many to use the method in order to catch a glimpse of what is going to happen in the near and distant future. At a time when the future is so unpredictable, managers and their consultants are receptive to procedures that promise to reduce uncertainty. These procedures range from sophisticated scenario techniques to the most diverse practices of fortune telling.

1.6.1 Constellation work – a present-day oracle?

Because the system constellation targets the underlying dispositions of a specific practice - you could say, of its DNA - it offers details of the next consistent step for an adequate further development of a system. It therefore does not forecast a certain future, but points to *sensible next steps that can be taken to cope with a precise task*.

In this regard the system constellation is no oracle. It does not relieve management from taking decisions, nor does it assure management that certain results can be met. On the other hand, it promotes discussion about decision-making premises. It contributes to managing complex problems. It points to the mechanisms that make up the dynamics of an organization and also promotes a culture of reflection.

It is related more closely to the theatre than to the oracle. As in theatre a space is set up that gains meaning through the presence and movements of the actors. Knowledge, whether corporate or private, in the original as well as in the enlightened form of the theatre, displays itself in scenes under changing titles. This knowledge is partly explicit and partly implicit. Both theatre and constellation work offer clues about the implicit knowledge of social systems by demonstrating it *without* making it explicit and thus questionable. The uniqueness and fascination of both media are established in this.

1.6.2 The validity of the images of a constellation

Every diagnostic method has to ask the question about where its validity lies. It has to clarify the relationship between the original or real phenomenon and its image. Or put another way: what can a manager, who is using the system constellation to solve problems and as a method to make decisions, truly rely on? As has been briefly mentioned already, the constellation picks up what is in the world of experience. Experience is inscribed in an organism and coordinates its movement towards a specific objective. It is and remains, however, invisible and manifests itself exclusively in the implementation of an action. By way of reflection it comes across to the interested players as "know-how". In the reflection itself there remain of course only *impressions* of the experience.

It would be an embarrassing mistake to confuse these impressions with the experience itself. Therefore, it would also be absurd to want to transfer the closing picture of a system constellation unchanged into a real system. That would be nothing more than a superficial "copy paste" procedure. That is just not what constellation work is about. It is about skilled "trackers" to whom a whole world is revealed from carefully observing the order of the tracks.

To use an analogy from the performing arts: the artist merges into his work indeed metaphorically speaking, but never recurs "in bodily form" in his work. The limit of representation is generally marked by this. The representation is the "impression", as it were, of the representative, but never the represented element itself. The track in the snow is not the fleeing animal, the portrait is not the person and the menu is not the food. Despite this there are of course equivalences, but they are on a *structural* level. Precisely this structural dimension is brought to the fore by the constellation work. We have just touched on several topics that are the domain of the theory of science and knowledge. We will take them up and differentiate them in chapter 2.

1.6.3 System constellation and management systems

We should like to close this chapter by pointing out an important difference between the system constellation and current management tools such as, budgeting. The latter is focussed on (highly abstract) "impressions" of a live business practice, namely on its numerical data. Whoever does this pays a price. He can no longer grasp the precise individual circumstances of the company. The activities of the company are transformed to some extent into a new aggregate state far removed from the original state. In recent years therefore doubts have arisen about whether current financial accounting adequately gives a true picture of a company that corresponds to the facts. As we have seen, the system constellation focuses also on a structural level, *without however suppressing the precise circumstances*. It always creates a relationship to a precise situation and for this reason to a precise practice. This is also one of its strengths. Consequently, as a procedure it applies *direct incentives for action* – in contrast to conventional management tools. The *concentration* of the basic aspects of a situation into a moving picture permits the information gained to be very easily retrieved. The participants will remember for a long time the body perceptions of their individual roles. The sequences of images continue to remain in their memories. This gives a system constellation the power of a vision that stimulates one to act immediately. It does not of course replace decision making processes. It does not make discussions with colleagues – even the difficult ones (!) – unnecessary. And personnel decisions should be made using traditional methods and procedures. To make it clear once again: system constellation is no (present-day) oracle.

CHAPTER 2

THE MURMURING OF IMPLICIT KNOWLEDGE

"Knowledge" is one of the concepts we like to speak about nowadays. As members of a "knowledge-based society" we owe it to ourselves to bring "knowledge" into our conversation at various opportunities. But the attentive listener soon notices that the word circulates with the most diverse meanings. Whenever one asks what is meant exactly by "knowledge", one becomes embarrassed as a general rule. That is however very strange. Although we all know quite a lot we cannot usually explain spontaneously what this knowledge is exactly!

Furthermore we shall concern ourselves in more detail with the dynamic aspect of knowledge. We understand by this that experience follows certain patterns. We shall also illustrate that every type of knowledge has another side that cannot be expressed, documented or even explained. That does not mean that this "tacit" knowledge would not be relevant for practice, quite the opposite: every type of expertise lives to a large extent from this aspect of knowledge. It is certainly very difficult to come by this knowledge by using only the usual diagnostic methods. This is because you cannot easily "capture" it with the three traditional codes – language, data and images.

If we take such a dynamic concept of knowledge as a basis, then we have to include a few things about which we will give more details in the following paragraphs. For example knowledge is a productive power, a resource to cope with our daily experience. There is a direct connection between knowledge and the "order of things" (Foucault 1966).

At the same time we shall take up the assertion in chapter 1 again and explain in more detail that this knowledge can be developed with the help of the system constellation. This should make plain once again what benefit accrues to management from constellation work.

2.1 Implicit and explicit knowledge

Present-day knowledge management has given us a vast amount of data. An extremely powerful computer technology has made light work of gathering, processing and administering data.

In the meantime, we have recognised that data only make sense and merge into knowledge if it can be integrated with the horizon of meaning and experience. If the management of knowledge is concentrated unilaterally on the management of data, then the horizons of meaning and experience, in which the players of a community of practice participate, soon become a limiting factor. Or put more bluntly: there is too much data and too little knowledge. A manager once described this discrepancy as follows: "Management systems are generally designed to offer too much information and that usually too late." Effective knowledge management thus means that only such knowledge is activated as is relevant for subsequent decision making and action.

However, let's return to know-how. It is difficult to acquire "experience" because a large part of it is to be found in our unconscious. Expertise, excellence or real skills, whether in the case of individuals, teams or complete organizations, are difficult to express in language, data or images. This means nothing more than that our current codes are clearly not sufficient to understand and adequately display what matters in a successful professional activity. It appears as if the "real" talent eludes any kind of claim by some form of "traditional" knowledge management.

Michael Polanyi used the concept of implicit knowledge for the first time relating to his theory of knowledge and perception. He assumed that intelligence is already present in mere action. He thought that action was not managed by some external instance where intelligence resides. For example it is not the head that controls the hand that reaches for the fork. The hand grasps the fork on its own to a certain extent. All complex processes for implementing a specific intention elapse without drawing on the intellect. Polanyi describes these complex processes "inscribed" on the body as "implicit knowledge". Implicit knowledge is of course at our disposal, but we do not develop a conceptual understanding for it as a rule. This always becomes clear whenever we can't find an answer to the questions "How exactly do you ...?" related to a skill or excellence. Somehow we seem to know more than we are able to express (Polanyi 1985). Although his work continues to circle around the phenomenon of implicit knowledge, the concept itself is not at the centre of Polanyi's work. This is different with Ikuijro Nonaka and Hirotaka Takeuchi and their basic contribution to knowledge management. In their book "The knowledge-creating company" this concept takes up a central role when looking for an answer to the question how knowledge is created in a company (Nonaka and Takeuchi 1997): "It is doubtless important to understand how a company develops new products, new methods and new organizational styles. But the more fundamental question is *how* do companies create new knowledge that makes these developments possible."

The authors equate implicit knowledge practically with subjective know-how gained from experience and dissociate it from objective or explicit knowledge. By explicit knowledge they understand that what we can recall from some "storage" – be it from memory, be it from some other source. They want to find out how individual expertise – that is the "knowing how" of individuals – is made available for the organization as a whole. Their concept rests on the presupposition that knowledge is created and expanded by interaction between the areas of implicit knowledge and explicit knowledge. On this basis, they are constructing a dynamic model of the transformation of knowledge. They affirm to have formulated an essential – perhaps the central – postulate of knowledge management: an answer to the question about how knowledge is created in organizations.

2.2 Renunciation of the magic of the stored knowledge

In addition to the sum of theoretical knowledge, knowledge also encompasses practical everyday rules and guidelines for behavior. This is how Probst, Raub and Romhardt (1997, p. 22) define knowledge in the standard work on knowledge management. That knowledge is supposed to have something to do with rules may at first perhaps appear strange. This is because it usually comes to us spontaneously that knowledge is "stored" in books, libraries or electronic data banks and we hope that these collections would treasure the "beautiful, true and good things" and thus would serve as a kind of emergency supply for difficult times. From these sources of factual knowledge, of "knowing that" – we think of retrieving what we need so that things proceed "safely".

However we have to state that everything that we hear and see daily has a similar quality to these "stored" elements of data banks. It appears wherever we turn as if we would be surrounded by millions of "factors" that influence us. As if the whole world would be nothing more than an overabundance of stimuli that are only waiting to be decoded.

Admittedly not everything that attracts our attention is relevant for us. Out of the multitude of details that surround us we choose those in a precise situation that appear to mean something to us. From the raw material of individual data we produce information by allocating importance. For the time being we create order. The chaos surrounding us becomes "comprehensible". What has all this to do with knowledge? We believe there is a very direct relationship: we give meaning to the sensory perceptions in a very *systematic way*. This way is concerned with the knowledge concept that we take as a basis for constellation work. On this understanding knowledge is not statistical – a pile of data – but something extremely dynamic.

Knowledge is a way, based on rules, that gives meaning to "pure" facts in a specific situation so that the next move towards an intended target, an objective or intention can take place.

2.3 From data to knowledge – and back again

Data therefore is not yet knowledge. It must first of all be made "alive". That is, it has to be placed in a meaningful relationship. This does not simply exist "by itself" as it were; it always relates to a precise observer. Data is only important when seen from the observer's point of view.

An observer turns data into information, or, as Gregory Bateson put it, "Differences that make a difference" (Bateson 1985). In his introduction to systemic management of knowledge, Helmut Willke points out that information is only then available "if an observing system uses specific criteria to ascribe relevance to a set of data" (Willke 2004, p. 31).

Our knowledge also plays a role in the way we accord meaning to data. Willke records further that "knowledge comes by integrating information in the context of our experience," (ibid. p. 34). Every individual, team or company understands things according to their vision of the world. This is characterized and gradually substantiated by all the experiences made during their existence. The substantiation takes place in the most diverse way: repeated consistent experience and theories are the means of reaching such substantiation. Knowledge also is connected with the formation, reproduction and modification of an organization.

For this reason, knowledge cannot really be equated only to theory. Knowledge is a practice that is originated and confirmed by communication (ibid. p.

33). A short example illustrates this "movement" between data, information and knowledge.

A list with figures and concepts – that is with data – is not worth the paper it is written on. It is only of value to the person studying it. The list is set out in various columns of figures and words like "turnover", "profit margin 1" and "profit margin 2" as well as "variation compared to previous year". Depending on their function in the company – and that also means depending on their knowledge and experience horizon – people have diverse relevance criteria. As a result the same data "initiates" different information in the hands of various "observers". And not only this:

The observers draw different conclusions from the information that lead to different actions. They legitimise these with their own specific knowledge. For example, the person responsible for marketing draws very different conclusions from the same list and pursues different objectives as for example a production manageress.

2.4 Knowledge as a complex testing operation – the structuring agents of organizations

A definition of knowledge as "knowing how" is compatible without any doubt with the more recent concepts of knowledge management based on communications theory. The latter understand knowledge as a process or, as described by Niklas Luhmann, as a "complex testing operation". This complex testing procedure can make handling information either easy or difficult. Knowledge is what is structurally available in current operations in order to clarify the question which difference makes a difference. Put simply; knowledge is the way individuals, teams or organizations perceive, test and thus understand something in order to come to terms with their everyday life. It is not necessary to specially activate knowledge: it is always involved in processing information from significant data. Knowledge is accordingly a very specific form of practice based on experience.

As mentioned, this experience is structured: it tends towards the formation of patterns. Patterns are originated and conserved according to specific *rules*. Experience and patterns are indeed merely two aspects of the same situation. Patterns give a coherent shape to everyday life and direct it towards the achievement of specific effects and results.

From here a bridge can be built to the structuring agents of social systems. Structuring agents constantly wrest clear, well-arranged relationships from chaos, i.e., "organization". In other words, they hold the world of the organization together. An organization cannot survive without structuring agents. They are something like the rules that give order to a game. Knowledge emerges as a condensate of collective experience from this system of rules. At the same time, knowledge creates orientation, team spirit and brings about a sense of identity.

A specific type of knowledge comes into play under the caption "structuring agents": social or organizational knowledge. Without wanting to decide the matter of dispute, whether there is in fact any knowledge *of the* organization or whether knowledge is assigned only to individuals in organizations, we briefly discuss the concepts "individual" and "social knowledge" in the following pages and refer to the interaction between these two.

Individual knowledge as well as individual abilities and skills are constantly activated by the expectations of a social context. To do something sensible together with others means nothing more than conforming to the expectations that are latently present or explicitly clear in a specific situation. According to Dirk Baecker however the sum of fulfilled expectations - resulting from all the "moves" rehearsed together and forming the daily practice – that are continually directed at individuals, is nothing more than *social knowledge*. The complex interaction between the knowledge that "is in our heads" and the knowledge that is "in the relationships" can be understood as a structural coupling (Baecker 1999, p. 65 ff). Both types of knowledge which in fact are quite difficult to distinguish unfold in a co-evolutionary process.

Referring to a company, that means all employees activate and develop precisely those competencies they need to cope with their everyday work. This everyday work conforms, however, over time precisely to the available abilities and skills. Precisely this circularity makes cultural development into a protracted business. Interventions into the system of basic rules are almost always sharply sanctioned. Well-meant appeals, on the other hand, are simply ignored.

2.4.1 Excursus: what holds an organization together?

What exactly then are these structuring agents and how do they work? Structuring agents form diverse patterns (Rüegg-Stürm 2002, p. 23 and 37 ff). They are however not completely inflexible but gradually change during the

various development stages of an organization. Because even if the members follow a rule, larger or smaller divergences from the rule are bound to take place. If these divergences assert themselves, because for instance they increase the chances of success, they gradually become new rules.

In his conceptualization of structuring agents of an organization, Rüegg-Stürm is following the ideas of Anthony Giddens (Giddens 1995): "In accordance with the concept of duality of structure, the structuring agents of social systems are both the means and result of the methods they organise recursively." This is how Giddens describes the interplay of rules and practice in his main work. The patterns and system of rules that constitute an organization, are in a mutual relationship. As a result organization is not something static, but a movement. As a result, the rules and their precise implementation mutually influence each other (Graph. 2).

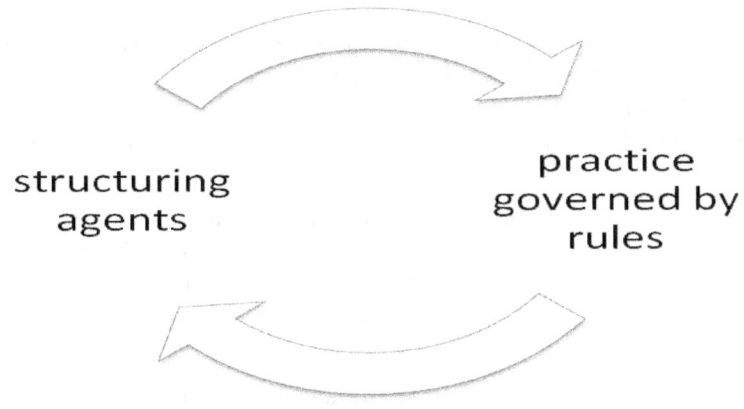

Graph. 2: *Circular structure of organization*

Depending on the line of vision, from which these structuring agents are seen, various dimensions can be recognized. The kind of differentiation of the structuring agents that Rüegg-Stürm carries out with the St. Gallen management model corresponds essentially to a triad that has become established in the theory and practice of management. He also uses the concepts strategy, structure and culture.

Strategic orientation

Strategies contain knowledge that imparts orientation. This strategic orientation knowledge helps the activities inside a company to be geared towards those aspects that are decisive for success. In addition, strategies also contain knowledge about the internal and external potential still to be implemented.

This potential is always exploited anew via routine activities.

Day-to-day action also claims a strategy as a kind of fixed or focal point in order to focus on it constantly. Therefore the call regularly sounds for a binding strategy in many an organization, especially in times of change. Due to the strategy everyone knows how to conduct daily business the "right" way, that is, with the best chance of success. A strategy absorbs insecurity, for all the players involved. Therefore you could say that strategies are a system of rules that establish on which fields the activities of an organization have to refer to and which resources are available in the process with a view to future success.

Coherent structures

Structures see to it that the mutual expectations of the managers and employees, who have to "collaborate", are not always disappointed. They are reflected in the "setting-up of the team". From this everyone can deduce the rules of the role-play with their promising basic moves and respective responsibilities.

The structure specifies the helpful and useful standard behaviour of the individual players. At the same time however it is consolidated by the recurring behaviour patterns. It preserves coherence. Coherent structures are the result of coordination procedures and at the same time they determine for their part the procedures of coordination.

As can be seen from this definition, Rüegg-Stürm means by "structure" not only those aspects called hierarchical structure and operational structure that find their (explicit) expression in organograms and process diagrams. He is also interested in the process of structuring (Rüegg-Stürm 2002, p. 53): "Order or organization is the result (...) of structuring processes to which a large number of people have contributed in very different ways and to a varying extent." For their part these processes follow their own patterns. Rüegg-Stürm describes them as "established structures" that directly restrict the scope for the development of a company. Many a manager engaged in a change process has had an unpleasant experience with rigid established structures whenever the proposed new organization was perceived as "imposed" and rejected by the parties concerned.

A connection can be made from the concept of "structure", to the proposition that organizations are systems of patterns whose development is guided by rules. Structures are a system of rules that:

- on the one hand constitute an appropriate division of labour and thus make efficiency and productivity gains possible,
- on the other hand make sure that the various activities are coordinated and integrated into a whole (ibid. p. 48 f).

This understanding of structure comprises a dynamic that cannot be described in organograms and process diagrams. This way structure is understood as a dynamic balance between the rules that govern the working relationships and the actual practise of the latter.

Culture: the shared horizon of reason

Within the framework of the structuring agents an identity of the company gradually develops that preserves a shared horizon of reason. Just as with traditional management literature, Rüegg-Stürm describes this aspect with the concept of "culture".

Only an attitude that appears meaningful can be generated - "mobilized" – in organizations on a sustained basis. If individuals, teams or organizations do not recognise themselves in some way in what they do, they will become less committed. Meaning is thus a powerful resource for creating and preserving coherence and continuity.

Culture is, as it were, the home of the ideologies that are valid in an organization. The standard answers to basic questions can be found there, for example:

- what do we want to achieve in the world?
- what are we capable of?
- how do we treat our customers?
- what do we think of our employees, colleagues and bosses?

For their part, these standard answers follow a specific logic and gradually merge into theories. We always access these theories whenever specific assessments and activities have to be legitimized for ourselves or others.

However, not only are the theories part of the culture. The sundry forms of materialisation inside an organization are also part of this. The luxurious headquarters or the bare manufacturing site are manifestations of a specific culture sculptured in stone or cast in steel and cement. However, culture also assumes its very specific shape in the configuration of the working areas, how it the company is portrayed in relation to its customers and quite generally in the many inconspicuous things that "enrich" everyday working life.

2.5 Rules and routines

As is clear from what we have said, structuring agents shape all communication and activity – that is all interpersonal and social events – in an organization. From these a microstructure of recipes for specific situations as well as traditions for behaviour and action gradually arise. These create a horizon of expectations that gives meaning to the activities of the participants and integrates them in a "natural" way (ibid. p. 61):

If similar recurring tasks and challenges are implemented and processed referring to the structuring agents, typical communications and behavioral patterns gradually develop for each business venture. Then we speak of a routinisation of the organizational flow of activity. The development of the structuring agents strategy, structure and culture and the routinisation of the organization's flow of activity are both sides of the same coin.

While one side of the coin gives an indication of the whole system of rules of the organization, the other side represents the events and routines that are observed and experienced in the everyday life of the organization. Both sides need each other. They are in a recursive relationship to each other. A cursory glance at the organization merely falls, however, on a single event and not on what basically causes this.

This system of rules cannot always be completely recognized. Usually only a part of it is written out in full. This is then preserved in guidelines, handbooks, work procedures etc. The much larger part of rules is largely obscure. They are part of implicit knowledge and have an effect without the players being aware of it. They control the players behind their backs. "That is simply done this way ...", is the answer to the question for which reason something is done in a very specific way and not in another. Continuing to insist on the "why?" and "how exactly?" usually cause a certain amount of embarrassment.

At first there are no dramatic consequences from the fact that the structuring agents are only partly conscious because everyone takes part. "One" simply follows the rules also because one has experienced that "automatically" following the rules offers a certain relief: it increases the mutual trust.

Difficulties always surface whenever something new is being tried, especially in the case of organizational changes. Then new rules clash with established rules and, as part of the established rules is complied with unconsciously, the "old order" prevails. On top of this, the new rules are unclear or challenged by some of the players because they have still not been agreed. In other words "Yes, we want changes of course, but the let's continue with the old ways!"

This could be the catch-22 situation that leads to logjams.

2.6 Rules in social systems

The strict focus on results often leads to a vague feeling rather than a clear awareness among the management when they have to deal with complex situations. The interplay of basic rules attracts little attention in daily practice and what we called "culture" it is less critically analyzed.

The contribution of these rules for the survival of the company as an autonomous unit is undervalued. Sometimes individual players use these rules to succeed with their own interests. In such cases of course they are careful to keep quiet about it.

It is worthwhile to look at what we call rules in still a little more detail. Because rules are not simply rules. Even with regard to their effect there are significant differences in form, importance and ambit. These deserve attention also with regard to a reflected "management of the system of rules".

In the following pages we therefore mention briefly the different effective force of rules. On the basis of Edward T. Halls' anthropological studies Fritz B. Simon distinguishes three levels of rules: grammatical, informal and technical rules (Simon 2004, p. 231 ff).

2.6.1 Grammatical rules

It is assumed that grammatical rules are to be observed. Their purpose is not questioned. Everyone knows without reflecting or discussing at length what is right and what is wrong, what should be done and what should not. The infringement of grammatical rules is penalized and when someone has "dropped a clanger" the emotive reactions become apparent.

Such rules become second nature within the context of socialization procedures. The mother language is cited time and again as an example for grammatical rules. Without having to know the rules, we use them usually without making errors.

At the same time, the scope of these rules marks the limit of the affiliation. Whoever constantly infringes grammatical rules, risks being excluded. Grammatical rules are internalizes, as it were, by trial and error. They effect the closure of a system and cater for a high degree of trust with those involved.

Grammatical rules induce feedback loops and consequently preserve the structure (ibid. p. 235): "Such rules only change slowly; their patterns represent tradition. They are inflexible, rigid and durable. Above all, they sustain the identity of the system and its participants."

2.6.2 Informal rules

Unlike grammatical rules informal rules offer a greater scope for options. What is judged to be wrong and what right is not so clear-cut and clearly defined. There are no clear-cut reactions to discrepancies. These too turn out not to be so intense. Positive feedback loops focus attention on what should be. The rules are internalizes correspondingly by imitating promising behavioral patterns. As informal rules are mostly more short-lived than grammatical rules, they do not sustain identity. For the latter they can be in a complementary, neutral or conflict-laden relationship.

Both kinds of rules implicitly "follow the prevailing current" and are therefore not, or only slightly, conscious, but that in no way diminishes their effect. The patterns they induced – we could also speak of structures, routines, methods or habits – proceed unsighted, self-organized and are subject to evolutionary principles. If we speak about these rules, it is usually perceived as a nuisance and is in any case risky to some extent.

2.6.3 Technical rules

The technical rules on the other hand are different. They establish the procedures by which agreed objectives should be achieved. They are part of explicit knowledge and accordingly can be expressed openly. Accordingly these rules were passed on in discussions, instructions or also training sessions. Consequently alternatives to a specific rule can be suggested and discussed. Technical rules offer explicit guidance for precise behavior.

Technical rules can be implemented or overruled reasonably quickly. This is solely a question of decision making and implementation and makes technical rules into a preferential "tool" of management based on an "engineering model". Even strategic programmes are based in most cases on the level of technical rules. This makes them prone to the "shallows" and "unplumbed depths" of that dimension in which grammatical and informal rules take effect.

2.7 System constellation as a receptor for implicit social knowledge

On the basis of our preceding deliberations, we can now understand more clearly just what a system constellation can achieve. This has given us a technique that enables us to spot the structures behind the facts that shape the circumstances in individual cases. This is a code that can express what we have described on the level of the individual as "expertise" and on the level of the organization as "excellence". Both have a lot to do with experience.

It seems to be a paradox that experience in times of constant change is a factor for success. Nevertheless, experience enables us to make a first move in difficult and confusing situations. *Experience gives us security.* Knowledge, on the other hand, leads if anything to discussions, doubts and complex analyses or to grandiose moves that nobody really trusts. Indeed experience can be disclaimed, but it cannot be denied. Doubt, on the other hand, is inherent in theoretical knowledge. Therefore in organizations often what is regarded as "fact" or "reality" has to be "negotiated". "Pure" expertise has a hard time being recognized.

System constellation inevitably relies on experience as it endeavours to formulate an image of a specific constellation and "find out about" the specific quality of the constellation via the experience of the representatives. This is possible because everyone has at his disposal a sensibility for perception of situational qualities (Schlötter 2005). The whole body participates in this perception, a process we can also call "intuition". This "sixth sense" unites us with the hidden structural elements of a situation – whether these have arisen "by chance" from the spontaneous movements of the representatives, or by deliberate interventions of the facilitator. It could also be formulated as follows: the system constellation endows intuition with "language" or expression. That has specific implications. The weak signals coming from our intuition can be transformed into data that become reliable information by means of a code – the system constellation. The method is thus completely new.

Whereas Ikuijro Nonaka and Hirotaka Takeuchi specify individual knowledge and develop concepts that specify how to collectivize this knowledge, constellation work in a management context focuses on *social intelligence*. Attention is turned especially to the implicit aspects. The constellation throws light on expectation horizons, common patterns or structures that establish the foundation of a specific practice and is to be found at the core of every organizational accomplishment. The system constellation gives observers a clear view of the basic set of rules of social systems. Graph. 3 narrows down again the area of the system constellation in the context of management.

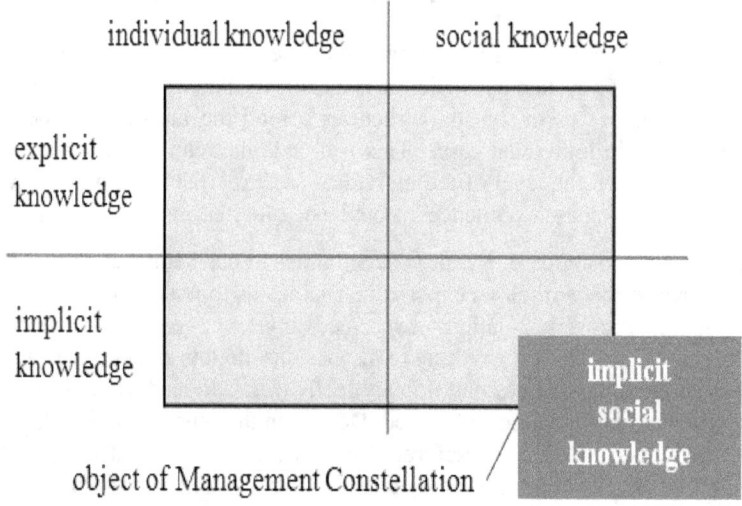

Graph. 3: Area of the system constellation in management contexts

As a result the system constellation captures implicit social knowledge as a kind of "fourth code" that can adequately break down such data that emerge principally via the intuition of the representatives. This takes place when the system constellation reproduces a precise situation in the room and the logic of this constellation is experienced on an affective – physical level by representatives "stepping inside" the constellation. This way it widens the scope of our knowledge base crucially including the emotional and intentional dimension.

System constellations open the management's eyes for the implicit orders as described above. They direct their gaze away from the "pure" focus on results, expressed in figures, to the dynamics that appear to "generate" these results. In doing so, they offer direct visual instruction. The representatives present the moves spatially. The "system" suddenly becomes clear. It acquires a tangible shape.

Management constellations make concepts of systems theory and communication theory available to management. Abstract concepts such as "business culture", "social intelligence" or "excellence" are crammed with life by comprehensive visual aids. For example, it also becomes clear why strategic programmes and structural defaults occasionally have no impact, even if a larger ring of stakeholders has developed and approved them. Because these defaults are nothing more than a cluster of technical rules that in the best case are unambiguous. They only take effect whenever they join the grammatical and informal system of rules, or whenever they serve as a helpful expedient when grammatical and informal rules are conflicting and lead to permanent confusion among the players concerned.

In addition, the system constellation allows a dual view of the actual situation of organizations. It sheds light not only on its precise development, but also the conditions of its potential. This makes it interesting for managers because it points to a second design level: to the system of rules or the framework for certain actions. With the help of a system constellation managers can manage the system of rules in a reflected way for developing, designing and directing their organizations. The potential of such a "Management of Rules" in order to increase the effectiveness of an organization is yet not fully exploited. This dimension is inevitably lost from sight due to the excessive focus on immediate results and the daily hustle and bustle. The design of the form is neglected by focussing purely on content.

The crucial advantage of the system constellation for management can be found here: indeed it directs attention away from the mere contents and instead to the dynamics inside and between the structuring agents, in other words, to what makes success possible beyond the intentions. But at the same time it preserves the contents and thus the solutions developed can become part of the practice that has been handed down.

Constellation sample: "abandoning" the "Strategic Intent"

The following description of a series of constellations with a management team developing and implementing a strategy in the course of something like more than half a year illustrates what has been said above.

With the help of a constellation it was examined what acceptability a mutually developed and recently implemented strategic intent, a strategy paper several pages long, had already found inside the management team. The leader in particular had his doubts about this – as expressed by his famous gut feeling – and he really wanted to find out whether his unease had been justified. The disillusion was huge: the constellation clearly indicated that the company (and also the members of the management team) were driven in particular by specific orders of key customers and not by the strategic intent. Accordingly the organizational practices were directed towards meeting the precise wishes of the customers. At an operational level everything appeared chaotic. The responsible people and organizational units clearly reached the limits of their capability. And nevertheless the demands of the customers drove them to give their best and they were proud that, in spite of everything, they had managed it once again – no matter what the cost.

The members of the management team were quite simply speechless to begin with. The irritation was so great that it was not possible to mutually draw consequences from the knowledge just gained. But one thing had become apparent: the daily routines had obviously created a culture with local theories that did not allow middle level management and the employees around them to engage with the contents of a new strategy.

Two months later the leader proudly presented several posters that showed important stages of the company's development. The series of diagrams with their characteristic scenes of day-to-day business pointed to the future rather than the past. The strategic intent and the potential it evoked had been given a face and origin! At various events, managers and employees had filed past the "pictures of an exhibition" and had spoken about the values that had in fact guided them.

After some time, a further constellation confirmed the supposition that the new strategy in its early phase had offered no binding frame of reference. The project that should create a standardised product line and implement the new strategy threatened to be shipwrecked miserably. The constellation shed light on the causes of the failure. It conveyed an image resembling a procession of mourners. Among other things it showed that hardly anyone had the project in mind and those responsible for the project had little support from the management team. There was therefore obviously a silent conflict regarding the basic strategic objective. In the discussion following the constellation, the diverse points of view of the members of the management team were discussed openly for the first time. During this discussion they also debated possibilities to defer the radical standardization in favour of intensive teamwork with key customers in product development.

This was the first time that the management were ready to discuss the structuring agents of their company. Because of the constellation work, they could now enter into a substantial discussion on the various aspects of the business culture. In doing so, that feeling of helplessness did not crop up as it usually does when discussing questions of the normative level.

PART II

GUIDELINES FOR CONSTELLATION WORK IN

MANAGEMENT CONTEXTS

Part II - Guidelines for constellation work in management contexts

In this part of the book we offer an overview of the system constellation's technique. We concentrate on their specific use as *Management Constellation* i.e., the work in team settings dealing with management topics. We suggest the relevant theoretical fundamentals, the methodical moves and technical "tricks" that have stood the test of time. These guidelines are aimed at consultants, who are already familiar with the technique of system constellations but would like to know more about its application in management contexts.

In chapter 3, we introduce principles that inform the development of social systems in general that are also valid for organizations. In chapter 4 we shall speak about the procedure of the system constellation and clarify questions regarding the three likely settings for constellation work. In chapter 5, we shall describe the individual phases of the standard course of a constellation with all that goes with it. In chapter 6 we offer an overview of some theoretical models that form the basis of the formats we use for constellation work. Part II closes with chapter 7 that briefly describes those methods with whose help we frame the actual constellation work.

CHAPTER 3

MOMENTS OF SUCCESS

While reflecting on the experience with system constellations (Bert Hellinger, Gunthard Weber etc.), basic principles, guiding the development of social systems, became clearer. Matthias Varga von Kibéd and Insa Sparrer deserve credit for having merged them into a standard theory. They cite four principles that we list here in order of their relevance for the growth and reproduction of social systems (Varga von Kibed and Sparrer 2000, p 170):

1. Observance of terms and conditions of membership,

2. Respect of seniority and priority,

3. Recognition of greater responsibility and commitment,

4. Development of individual performances and skills.

These principles offer a helpful basis for the interpretation of constellation images and the simulation of alternative constellations. As a general rule, experienced managers know about these principles intuitively. Nevertheless it is appropriate to refer to them explicitly so that managers can better understand the interventions during the constellation work.

3.1 Observation of the terms and conditions of membership

The observation of the terms and conditions of membership is of fundamental significance for the *existence and survival of the system*. First it must be clear who is part of a system and who is not. Dubious system boundaries create confusion and have a negative influence on the commitment of members. As a result, unproductive unease arises in the system.

Organizations define membership basically through a formal employment contract. But it must always be further defined by the description of the specific function assigned in the division of labour.

If clarification is omitted, corrosive forces develop that cannot be forestalled by repeatedly reaffirming the objectives to be achieved. The effect of basic rules is stronger than repeated requests.

Dismissals and replacements – not only of key functions – are therefore always critical moments that are not always given the necessary attention in companies. System constellations clearly show inconsistencies regarding membership and allow for the testing of measures that are necessary for the integration of new members or, if necessary, the dismissal of employees.

The terms and conditions of membership need special attention, whenever a project organization is superimposed on the line organization. System constellations showed that in complex forms of organization blockages can easily appear when the rules regarding membership, responsibilities and duties are not clear.

But also in the case of restructurings and acquisitions, it is advisable to take a look at the terms and conditions of membership. Relationships that are not transparent reinforce harassment tendencies and can make it impossible even for highly competent employees to be integrated into an organization. The topic of membership terms and conditions is also highly critical in the case of temporary management contracts.

3.2 Respect of seniority and priority

The second principle refers to the *development of systems*. There are two types of development: growth and reproduction. Appropriately, diverse basic rules are valid for each.

The basic principle of seniority is valid in social systems in the case of a growth dynamic. When new functions and personnel are added, the more senior employees' precedence must be recognized.

The following example illustrates the dynamics of this: a production manager could only implement new ideas and concepts that he had developed together with younger managers and a recently appointed specialist after his efforts had been duly approved by the more senior master craftsmen. Prior to this they did not want to acknowledge the innovations and held on obstinately to what they had done before.

The production manager picked up a hint about this in the course of a constellation. As it transpired, the older generation felt themselves pushed back by the younger generation. This dynamic was reinforced by the fact that to begin with the production manager had concentrated on the younger employees and had hardly taken any notice of the older ones, who of course offered deep-seated resistance to the proposed changes.

In connection with reproduction – e.g., in the case of setting up subsidiaries – the principle of inverse chronological order applies. The newly formed system takes precedence over the one already in existence.

New systems can only then gain their autonomy and unfold if they are equipped with appropriate resources and shielded against the claims of existing systems. We would like to illustrate this briefly with the help of an example:

The innovation process was redefined in a company. They were on the verge of launching the new concept, but saw themselves confronted by frictions among the functions involved. Things only got back to normal when *production management*, that had initiated the newly created process, had also in effect taken over management accountability and made this clear to the other parties involved. Now that the new unit had stated its autonomy the functions that had already been in the company for some time merged without any further problems into the "new" order. Also on this occasion a constellation had provided the decisive pointer.

3.3 Recognition of greater responsibility and commitment

The third principle concerns the rules that govern the network of relationships in a system:

The contribution of an employee or team or rather an organization unit for the overall good of the company has to be treated with proper consideration and appreciation.

Accepting responsibility and readiness for action benefit the stabilizing powers of an organization and sustain its relative autonomy in the face of its environment. Insa Sparrer uses the metaphor of immune power (Sparrer 2006, p. 51). In social systems "immune power corresponds to accepting responsibility and readiness for action."

The priority of greater commitment plays a central role. It is, as a rule, linked to the position inside a hierarchy. But occasionally an exceptional situation, for example a crisis, also exacts an extraordinary commitment from those concerned although they are not officially in charge. Both kinds of commitment have to be respected equally. In this connection, Sparrer corrects the demand of traditional organization theory that formal hierarchy has to take precedence over informal hierarchy (Sparrer 2001, p. 118): "The official hierarchy (...) tends to safeguard the external image of the organization. Consideration of the informal internal influences safeguards against sabotage,..."

Individuals and teams that provide a heavy commitment for an organization – founders and leaders as well as departments that embody key skills – have a right to greater influence. On the other hand, whenever personnel or departments make a claim to power that is not in proportion to their contribution for maintaining and developing the system, we can speak about a presumptuous action. The consequences are overwork and a decrease of effectiveness by of those who assume such a position, as well as inner withdrawal and resignation by those who have to carry the consequences of such a claim.

3.4 Development of individual performances and skills

The fourth principle refers to the individual development of personnel or subsystems. The differentiation of tasks and functions according to performance and skills inside social systems rests on this:

Higher performance and better skills must be rewarded appropriately.

Recognition of performance achieved improves motivation in general and appraisal of skills makes resources accessible. Equal treatment of different contributions is dysfunctional and in general leads to lower motivation and less willingness to learn.

This fourth principle is highly valued precisely in those organizations that are strongly performance-oriented. The other three basic rules are given less attention. If the higher principles are disregarded however, the whole system can become destabilized. For this reason, individual development has to be "embedded" in a framework of rules that contributes principally to safeguarding the existence and survival of the system, its development and autonomy. Without such a framework, individual development cannot take place.

CHAPTER 4

SETTINGS OF CONSTELLATION WORK

Systemic constellation work, in its original form, is a kind of group therapy led by a therapist in which clients deal with personal issues in a group. An "initial image" of the family system focuses on personal entanglements, obstacles or misplaced love. That image evolves through repositioning the representatives and ritual procedures to become a "solution image" that offers relief (Weber 1998, p. 11): "The past is linked to the present and future in a solution-oriented way." The closing image gradually unfolds its healing power after the constellation is terminated, just like a homeopathic cure. This applies especially to work with a therapeutic focus.

The first constellations on questions about work and organizational contexts borrowed the setting from therapeutic work. In "open" seminar groups clients raise their professional concerns. This setting offered, and still does, a safe framework for working on issues relating to *personal success* in a working context. Usually, in such constellations relational dynamics between people are prominent; the organizational aspects form a kind of background for the events contemplated.

On the other hand in the case of constellation work within a team, i.e., management constellations, this background itself becomes the main topic. The organization is the main subject. Aspects of relationships between individuals or issues of personal success are deliberately not addressed. The question is no longer: "How can I improve my role within the organization?", but: "What decisions must we take as a team so that the organization as a whole becomes (more) successful?" This change of perspective on its own asks for a decisive change in the way of working in the team setting.

Moreover questions relating to management contexts are essentially a matter of sense-making and not healing. In doing so, attention is paid not so much to the final image, but mainly to the process that leads to it. We affirm at this point that the process as a whole is relevant for establishing meaning. We shall go into this proposition in more detail in the chapter on future prospects at the end of this book.

Systemic constellation work is used regularly also in individual settings, that is in individual counselling, or coaching. The complete openness relating to the topics being processed is an essential advantage of this private setting. In addition to questions from the work context those of a personal nature can also be openly referred to if need be.

We shall go into the three diverse settings in more detail in the following sections and outline their specifications more precisely. We shall begin with a detailed description of the team setting, continue with the delineation of the "open" seminar form and finish with a description of work in individual settings.

4.1 Team Setting – Management Constellations

In the late 1990s, consultants started to use systemic constellations when working with a team inside companies for the first time. In doing so, they focussed both on relational dynamics between individual players and on very specific management questions such as the validation of strategic options, simulation of organizational changes, improvement of relationships between the individual stakeholders etc. In addition, they included managers, or rather employees, directly involved in a problem as representatives in the constellation work.

They used constellation formats such as those Gunthard Weber and other consultants had developed under the title *Organizationsaufstellungen* (Organizational constellations) and Insa Sparrer and Matthias Varga von Kibéd under the title *Systemische Strukturaufstellungen* (Systemic structural constellations).

In about 2000, together with other consultants the authors started to use system constellations in the course of consultancy. A specific intervention practice has gradually developed from this and was named "Management Constellations". These hark back to various formats of systemic constellations and combine them with the methods of the "Learning Organization" (Chris Argyris, Peter Senge, Claus Otto Scharmer etc.) as well as other systemic procedures like e.g., "Group-Field" (David Benz-Chartrand) and "Dialog" (David Bohm). This very specific kind of intervention practice makes tacit implicit knowledge (Michael Polanyi) accessible in development or change processes and leads to a new form of thinking and action through a controlled sense-making process (Karl E. Weick).

Management Constellations do not only make the underlying dispositions, or, it could also be said, the DNA, of a certain business practice *directly tangible and visible*. They also shed light on compatible steps for a consistent development of the company. They predict less an abstract future but rather provide evidence on how the team can *master a certain challenge on the basis of a system-inherent excellence*. This orientation towards a very practical and operational next step makes it easy for those people involved to develop *and* implement lasting solutions.

4.1.1 Constellation work in management contexts

The whole potential of the system constellation for internal use in an organization has only been partly explored so far. It is however only consistent to use other channels for access to implicit knowledge as such that impart explicit knowledge. Whoever endeavours such a change of approach, will gain surprising insights into the tacit knowledge of a company.

The system constellation uses the *body as a highly sensitive instrument for perception*. Some managers view this as a bit of a risk and those, who apply the system constellation for decision-making processes, are still in the minority.

Managers, who have been involved in this, specified benefits such as:

• System constellations focus attention on the relevant information. This is a stroke of luck at a time when a flood of data is constantly diverting attention from what is essential.

• In the case of constellation work surprising solutions often become visible. Using this method we can understand things much better.

Thereby new measures can be implemented more systematically and efficiently. Last but not least it also saves time and reduces costs.

• Using this method complex data can be diagnosed extremely quickly.

• The special form of visualization and body perception helps participants to remember the experience and the insights.

A special course of action is needed if the system constellation is to be integrated into consultancy practice in management contexts. It was not available when we started constellation work and only evolved gradually as more experience was gained by using the method in these very specific surroundings.

Below we outline and comment on the characteristics peculiar to the intervention practice of management constellations:

• the special purpose: topics relating to the organization, development and management of entire companies or corporate divisions,

• the special perspective: the questions of a whole management team,

• the special workshop design, that is based on the methods of the "Learning Organization",

• the special kind of inclusion: managers confronted with specific questions are also deployed as representatives,

• the special context: integration in a superordinate consulting or change process.

Purpose of Management Constellations

Management constellations focus their attention on all aspects that correspond to coping successfully with the tasks in the organization. Or put another way, they shed light on the central questions relating to management, such as organizing, developing and managing a company. For example, they keep an eye on interdependencies such as:

• the interdependence between the sales channel, existing marketing strategy, overall quality management, an innovation project and the sales target of a business division, or

• the correlation between the existing routines of production, the perfectionism of the skilled expert, a cost-cutting programme, an important supplier and the target return on investment.

The work relationships between the individual players are only just one of many possible (context) factors in the case of this comprehensive approach.

Right from the beginning, the facilitator of management constellations has to deal with a very complex and intricate situation. In addition, the various elements of these layers or dimensions are in all probability in latent conflict with each other. It is important therefore that the facilitator reduces this complexity to a manageable extent before he begins at all with the real constellation work. The topic with all its relevant facets is *modelled* for an impending system constellation.

For this first phase it is helpful to have a kind of map or a heuristic grid to hand that can offer guidance in the modelling process. Prior to the actual constellation, a management model makes this work easier. It helps the participants to establish a point of view, to formulate a relevant question and to clear the boundaries of the system. If this point is clarified, the model also makes it easy to discover the relevant elements to be set up (see also chapter 6).

Perspective and workshop design of management constellations

A further specific aspect of management constellations is defining the perspective, or, as expressed in the technical terminology of constellation work, the "focus" (M. Varga von Kibed / I. Sparrer).

In the conventional constellation the "focus" always stands for a precise point of view of an individual person or still more exactly that part of a person, involved in the specific topic that is being examined.

However, in the case of system constellations in work contexts a complete team usually produces a specific topic. The focus then does not represent an individual but a *collective perspective*. Already for this reason the constellation work has to be incorporated in a more comprehensive process, i.e., before and after the members of the management team have to engage in an exchange of views.

In the preparatory stage, it is indispensable to clarify in a "Dialogic Interview" (C.O. Scharmer), what the common concerns of the management team are. This phase is decisive. For example, with the help of systemic questions and an appropriate management model, it is necessary "to dissect" the topic. Further, the elements and boundaries of the system being reproduced have to be defined together with the management team.

The "immersion" of constellation work in a business context required further adjustments. In a therapeutic setting, it is generally seen as not very practical to discuss a constellation afterwards. Too much speaking could reduce the effect of the constellation on the client.

On the contrary, in a management context the discussion subsequent to a system constellation is extremely helpful. It provides the participants with an opportunity to exchange their perceptions as representatives or their views as observers. Such a discussion supports a "collectivization" of the various perspectives and perceptions that have been experienced in the course of a constellation by the different protagonists and observers. It leads to a mutual reflection and helps to assimilate the experience and to transform the insights into functional measures.

The "Dialogue" developed by David Bohm, is ideally suited for this type of mutual reflection. It helps to condense verbally the observations made during the constellation. Further new insights often emerge due to the characteristic attitude of participants suspending their own judgement, merging thoughts into a larger whole, paying attention to the nuances and also "voicing" what has been perceived on an emotional level. In the course of a "Dialogue", preliminary ideas for subsequent interventions in the organization can be expressed.

It is remarkable that the quality of the discussion after a constellation is very different than it is in discussions on the same topic beforehand. Evidently constellation work reminds the team members that different points of view can co-exist and that their own is not necessarily the only right one.

At the end of the discussion a member of the management team is given the task of ensuring that the topics to be processed are put on the management agenda and not forgotten.

The language used by the facilitator during the constellation work is a further element that gives this intervention practice its distinctive shape. He usually makes an effort to adopt a reflective attitude and does not retain the directive style that is often used in classic constellations. Accordingly the clients are more "reflective observers" than "deeply moved protagonists". For this reason constellation work forfeits a part of its suggestive power that is otherwise peculiar to a ritual. It becomes an intervention that, according to Simon, leads to reflection on how the system communicates (Weber, Schmidt and Simon 2005, p. 127).

Constellation work with those directly concerned

"Why should I dedicate three days of my time, if I can get the answer to my question in two hours?" This comment of a manager invited to a constellation seminar was at first discouraging, but it was honest and contained the elements of a new solution.

If very busy managers do not come to constellation work, then the constellation work will of course have to go to them. The constellation *for* organizations has to transform itself into the constellation *within* organizations. That sounded at first very obvious and simple. A wide variety of constellation formats had been developed. They just had to be put into practice! However a very serious obstacle stood in the way of realizing such an idea. There were authoritative voices among the (family) constellation practitioners who described it as improper to use the members of a social system as representatives in constellations. They felt those involved would not speak openly about their perceptions as representatives. It could in fact lead to an intentionally distorted message.

Initially, such warnings had their effect. Only very hesitantly did consultants, trained in constellation work, attempt to conduct constellations in organizations with those concerned. Admittedly, this had surprising success whenever, contrary to all apprehensions, a chance was taken, but on the one condition that only organizational topics and not relational dynamics between the team members were treated in the constellation. In this respect the original rule not to use those participants as representatives of themselves or colleagues in the constellation is still respected.

Integration in an intervention process

A single constellation as a special event definitely has its uses. It certainly amounts to a gain in knowledge. In addition, the participants always experienced the phenomenon of representative perception as fascinating. But the solution that emerges is implemented differently in organizations than it is in families for the very reason that basically both systems are focussed very differently. For this reason, a company's development is different from that of a family.

All this should be reflected in the relevant consultancy practice. Precisely in the case of strategic (or also comprehensive, operational) questions a well-structured change management is needed to transform constellation images into precise social practices. This forms a kind of framework for the various interventions that govern and support the change.

System constellations develop their full potential in this context only when repeated. They stimulate the activities of steering groups, as well as project teams. The episodes from single constellations that have led to interventions can be picked up again and discussed later, because it is always informative to investigate what change has been activated by an intervention (or perhaps not). In a serious discussion the participants can draw useful conclusions on how the organization's system of rules functions and how they are managed more effectively.

System constellations prove themselves to be especially useful by showing the dynamics that are perceived as barriers when strategies should be implemented. Often the technical rules for directing and organizing the company are either contradictory or in conflict with the basic grammatical rules of the organization. For this reason the implementation of new ideas can be resisted quickly. During the constellation the participants gain a new understanding of resistance and, what is important above all else for the managers, learn a new creative way of dealing with barriers. How often have constellations made clear that barriers contain the power of unused resources!

Management Constellations as a self-contained intervention practice

In a management context, constellation work has evolved into a tool that enables communication about the aspects of a situation that had not been accessible hitherto to the managers. It can no longer claim to solve the problem in a single intervention, but it can be associated intelligently with other tools of the company's or organization's development and gains something essential, such as transparency, in the process.

Another consequence of bringing constellation work into the organizations is working directly with those concerned. Their individual work relationships are not the focal point of discussions, but problematic aspects in connection with the division of labour. The constellation work is embedded in a dialogue and integrated in a change management process.

In the process, it has lost something of its original magic and of its guise as a kind of transitional ritual. One thing however has not changed. Constellation work allows us to take up what could best be described as the driving forces of the organization. Depending on the point of view this is described as an instance and then called "soul" or "spirit" (Bert Hellinger); or it is understood as the predisposition of our action and known as "implicit knowledge". The intention of constellation work has therefore remained the same. What has changed is the intervention practice known as Management Constellation.

4.2 "Open" seminars

At the beginning of the 1990s, Bert Hellinger transferred constellation work to larger social systems and organizations under the title *Organizationsaufstellung* (Organizational constellation). At about the same time Varga von Kibéd and Sparrer developed the systemic structural constellation (Sparrer and Varga von Kibéd 1998, p. 394): "It represents an extension of constellation procedures from the family system to other contexts."

Initially, they all used the setting of the "open" seminar. As a rule the seminars are open to the public. The seminar participants raise questions such as:
- why am I not very effective as manager, team leader or consultant?
- why are there always similar tensions in my team?
- why is there a constant turnover of staff in a certain position?
- how can I deal with a certain dilemma?
- what is stopping me from achieving my objectives?

"We have had the best experiences with (...-) groups, where 15 to 20 members came from the most varied work areas and organizations and did not know each other previously. Here everyone is protected and free and feels equal. Everyone can take part in a wide range of constellations and at the same time a wide range of possible solutions. For such (...-) seminars we think a time frame of 2–3 days would be best." (Weber and Gross 1998, p. 409.)

When experimenting with constellations on work related issues, personal problems always came to the fore with full force. It was not uncommon for what began as an organizational constellation to end up as a family constellation. Obviously constellation work contains a critical point that favours the transition into a new paradigm. Varga von Kibéd and Sparrer describe this phenomenon as a *change of structural level*. The facilitator can induce this change of level intentionally himself, by taking up the additional points of view that present themselves from a family perspective. Then he can, if previously agreed with the client and in the appropriate context, work effectively and to the benefit of the client. If the facilitator does not notice the change of level, the constellation can overburden the client or expose him embarrassingly in an inappropriate setting.

The phenomenon of the change of level or topic is well known to us in our everyday conversation. But we have several defence mechanisms that help us to avoid speaking about disagreeable subjects. System constellations obviously thwart these strategies.

One thing however made this peculiarity of constellation work clear. Work contexts obviously invite the players to repeat behavioral patterns that they have practised in the course of their socialization in his family, but that are not always appropriate in the prevailing situation. Such behavior is dysfunctional and is not conducive to the accomplishment of the tasks. In the way he focuses attention the person concerned is managed by the wrong programme.

If this is reprocessed and worked through carefully in an appropriate setting, perhaps in a self-awareness group using a system constellation, it amounts to an effective separation of contexts for the client:

• the sales engineer understands perhaps that his customers should appreciate him but are not forced to love him. They can never replace the parental love he never enjoyed.

• the gifted, young physicist no longer has to save "his" department that is facing a critical moment. He remembers the effort he made to safeguard his parents, who should really have been safeguarding him as a child.

• and the intelligent product manageress no longer has to appeal to "her" boss at any price. She is aware that daughters can simply be daughters and do not need to be better than their mothers.

The issues that can be addressed in open seminars are almost limitless. It is incumbent upon the facilitator to focus on the aspects listed in the tender of his seminar.

4.3 Individual setting

Most of the remarks made regarding team setting and open seminars also apply to the individual setting. The main difference lies in the method used to represent the elements. There are various alternatives that we will describe in the following chapters.

4.3.1 Constellation work at the table

If it is about integrating constellations in a coaching session post-it labels are an ideal aid. The basic advantage of this is that the client can use something with which he is familiar. Nobody would be annoyed if asked to note names or other details on a colored post-it label during the course of the discussion. This technique offers still more advantages:

• the sheet of paper with the representation of the system can be left on the table during a longer discussion. It can be referred to again and again and simulate new variations and options by changing the position of the post-it labels.

• the initial image, provisional result and/or final image can be recorded by photocopying or photographing it and left with the client at the end.

• if some grid or matrix is taken as a basis for the constellation (we comment on this technique further on in this section), it can be easily drawn on an A3 sheet of paper.

A constellation can also be set up at the table using objects that are just lying around or with special figurines or symbols. For example, Playmobil figures and chess pieces are well suited for this as are the specially produced pieces that for example Carl-Auer Verlag distributes. The three-dimensionality (in contrast to the two-dimensional post-its) makes it easier for some clients to associate with the figure presented and engage in the representative perception that produces its positioning in the system portrayed.

If objects that are available on the table or in the room are used, it often has the effect of an anchor to which reference can easily be made in the course of the procedure and in everyday life in order to evoke specific images and circumstances.

4.3.2 Constellation work in the room

It is preferable to set up a constellation in the room, if circumstances allow, especially in the case of complex topics. As in the seminar setting, the whole room is used. In this case people are not used as representatives, but markers are placed on the floor: a sheet of paper, a piece of felt or something similar. The client is invited to place the markers on the floor and so becomes completely involved in the constellation. He has to stand up, go to the spot where he wants to place the marker and so gets a feeling for the positions by placing the markers. The effect of the constellation is experienced intensively using this method. For some clients this makes it easier to link the cognitive, emotional and physiological levels of the experience together.

The changes in the course of the constellation process can have a more enduring effect if experienced by the whole body and not just by the hand. In addition, it is easier for some people to concentrate if they stand up and "lead" a marker to its exact spot.

If the coach has established a good contact and mutual trust, the coached can get involved in such an experiment without further ado. He asks them to place the markers in the room, in order to present his inner image of the relationships between these elements.

The coach can also position himself wherever he likes and disclose his body perceptions, emotions, thoughts and his motion impulses. Then he invites the client to take his place in the system. Now the effects of the changes can be tested. It is helpful and useful first of all to ask the client which relocations he would carry out and to make sure that he himself makes the first move.

The so-called cataleptic hand can be used to sound out the relationship to individual players in order to avoid a too frequent change from the role of coach to that of a representative that could confuse the client. The coach's "dissociated hand", positioned at eye level above the spot where the element would stand (cf. section 5.9), represents an element of the system in this technique, developed by Varga von Kibéd and Sparrer.

If the client is well centred or has already some experience in constellation work, he can try out the positions of other representatives. This could be helpful for him because in this way he learns to understand the positions of other actors better. Care has to be taken during the work that the client is not confused or overburdened by constant changes.

CHAPTER 5

THE SEQUENCE OF THE CONSTELLATION

In this chapter we list the sequence of the moves that make up a constellation. In doing so, we give several tips relating to the particular sequence that the facilitator could find useful.

5.1 About the role of the facilitator

Attentive and explicit contact with the team, transparency regarding the methods used as well as clarity about the agreed objective are preconditions for the successful co-creative process of the management constellation. A happy medium has to be found between the greatest possible abstinence at the content level and the highest possible presence at the process level; as well as between consciously controlling the process and openness for everything that is taking place at the moment. Generally speaking the following maxim holds true for the facilitator:

Accept your "not knowing" and look out for what the constellation has to offer!

That does not of course mean that a facilitator would not need to know the specific facts that characterise the situation the management team is facing. It is most useful if he is sufficiently familiar with current management and organizational concepts. This is indeed a sign of appreciation towards the client.

In addition, the effect of a consultancy service increases if the facilitator has a wide repertoire of methods available. Favorite interventions soon lose their impact and searching for the "only right tool" quickly triggers a healthy scepticism.

5.2 Framing the question

The first move of an organizational constellation is to make sure the question, to which an answer should be found, is worded precisely and clearly.

The following should be observed:
- what is the problem, or rather, what topic should the constellation tackle,
- for whom is the objective relevant and
- what consequences could result from the solution.

The more precisely and practically the initial question is worded, the more explicit the answer will be. However, intentionally worded non-specific questions can lead to new insights, but the intention has to be communicated clearly in order not to raise false expectations.

In a management constellation the topic usually concerns the whole team present, even if it is explicitly presented by a single person, perhaps the boss or the consultant himself. The consultant has to make sure that he is authorised by the whole group, and especially by the boss, to deal with the proposed topic.

5.3 Determining the elements needed for constellations

The choice of the elements that make up the constellation is one of the facilitator's most important duties. As we suspect the orientation of the learning process is not only set in the actual constellation work, but already in the sequences prior to that. Focussing depends, for example, on whether the constellation is used in order to confirm a chosen strategy (e.g., "How can we improve cooperation with our alliance partner?") or, in order to reflect critically on the premises of a decision (e.g., "Do we have the same interests as our alliance partner?"). For this reason alone it is worthwhile investing enough time for this phase.

In cooperation with the client, the facilitator determines what characteristics adequately describe a certain situation. This means that at least for the time being the remaining options will be excluded. The result of this move is a set of variables that reciprocate with each other. Constellation work then sheds light on the inherent dynamics between these variables.

The choice of the elements is the result of an iterative process. Depending on the question (e.g., How can we increase the number of innovations?) it comprises the following points:

- determining the perspective of observation – who is primarily interested in solving the problem?

Example: the manager responsible for product development, in order to satisfy the objectives of the CEO, and not the product manager.

- choosing the system boundaries or the segment – whom or what do we include in processing the problem?

Example: the product development and marketing department and not the clients or other departments of the company.

- choosing the logical level of observation – what are we looking for?

Example: for cooperation of the players participating in the innovation process and not for the structuring agents culture, structure and strategy and also not for objectives, barriers and resources.

- choosing the model that should describe and interpret the situation – what causal map, or rather, which set of variables forms the basis to our point of view?

Example: The organogram of the company and the St. Gallen Management Model and not the resource triangle.

System constellations in management contexts always include the following elements:

- the "focus", i.e., that function or rather organizational unit from whose point of view the topic is seen,

- an assignment, a duty or an objective,

- various players, i.e., functions, groups or organizational units that are involved in the situation as agents or participants,

- relevant context factors,

- sometimes also decision options.

"Focus" is the term suggested by Varga von Kibèd to indicate the representative for the main "player" in the constellation. The Management Constellation, as a rule, works with a "focus" that represents the views of the whole team, a so-called "team focus". In the case of severely diverging interests two or more "focuses" can be used for the various points of view.

It is important to keep the number of elements as small and manageable as possible. If the facilitator suspects that an important element would not be mentioned, he can have a representative present for "something that could perhaps be relevant". This can happen either at the start or during the course of the constellation.

When defining the elements, it is advisable to use the same concepts team members have used when describing the situation. In the case of concepts with a negative connotation, the facilitator should suggest neutral alternatives in order to make a reframing during the constellation easier.

If working with larger groups, it is appropriate to clarify the question and select the elements with only some of the group, e.g., in the fish bowl setting (section 7.5).

5.4 Selecting and positioning the representatives

In the case of Management Constellations, or rather in team-setting, the team can instruct one of its members to select and position the representatives. This team member then represents the whole team. If there are conflicting opinions in the team, it is advisable to have two or even three members of the team selected to set up the constellations together. Those delegated choose the representatives together and afterwards, in pairs or threesomes, they place them in an appropriate spot without speaking.

Ideally representatives should not be chosen from those who carry out those functions, e.g., the marketing manager should not be chosen as a representative for the marketing-mix. This avoids unnecessary mixings. In addition, it can be very stimulating if the controller represents the point of view of the marketing mix.

Moreover in Management Constellations it has proven very worthwhile to allow team members to find themselves the representation appropriate to them. The facilitator asks who among the workshop participants responds to a certain element and would like to represent it. The representatives then choose their own spot. This can take place simultaneously or sequentially.

A further possibility is to lay down place markers for the elements (perhaps colored pieces of felt) and to invite the participants to take up a position they feel attracted to. This technique also makes sense if there are not enough people to be representatives.

If a system about to be set up in a constellation has many elements, then the setting up can be done step by step. The facilitator has a selected number of representatives put in place. He interviews them and possibly carries out the first adjustment. Afterwards he lets other representatives take up their positions. This procedure allows all participants to gain a good overview.

In order to reduce the complexity of the constellation some representatives can be chosen, but for the time being not put in position. They pay attention to their perceptions like the representatives in position, but they remain seated at the margins of the constellation. They will be questioned from time to time and if required set up later on.

5.5 Interpretation of a constellation image

The facilitator focuses his attention on various aspects in the course of the constellation in order to grasp the qualities of the system represented. But he pays attention especially to the following facts:

• typical geometric patterns of the constellation and their effect on the representatives,

• conspicuous expressions and motion impulses of the representatives,

• posture of the representatives,

• his own body resonance in various places of the constellation.

Based on his interpretation of the constellation the facilitator continuously develops hypotheses on the dynamics that become manifest in the system represented with the help of the representatives' reactions. Table 1, based on the experiences of the constellation work hitherto, offers guidance on interpreting typical relationship patterns between two representatives.

Perspective		Line of sight - focusing	Intensity of the relationship
A	B	Same orientation but no or only poor common focusing	No or poor relation between the elements

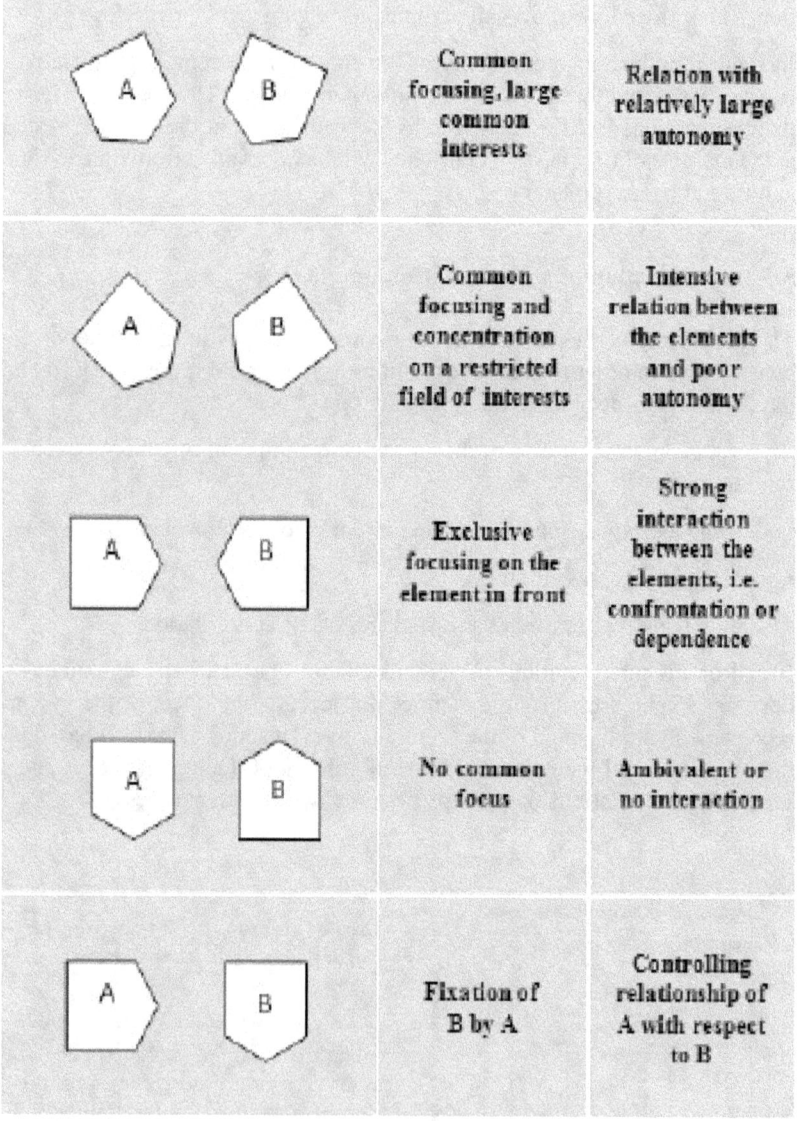

Tab. 1: Meaning of the angle and position in the constellation (in accordance with directions of Bert Hellinger and Gunthard Weber as well as Varga von Kibéd and Sparrer 2000, p. 171 ff)

The diagram above does not have a normative character. It offers the facilitator help by putting his hypotheses into words. At any rate, the main thing is to integrate the perceptions of the representatives into the formulation of the hypotheses. The lynchpin, in the case of actual work, lies in their body resonance.

Hypotheses, in the terms of provisional assumptions regarding a specific situation, guide the facilitator in his interventions. In order to make interventions understandable for workshop participants, it is useful to announce hypotheses openly and prompt workshop participants to introduce their own impressions and ideas.

It appears constellations are based on a kind of coordinate system that determines an order of precedence and chronological sequence. For this reason, in the final image the representative of the management team is standing usually on the right of the representative of an operational department and an important resource behind a specific representative. Figure 4 describes some typical possible interpretations of the positions of representatives. Depending on whether it is a matter of a relationship between the focus and a functional unit or between the focus and a value, or rather a resource, the interpretations listed in table 2 are possible.

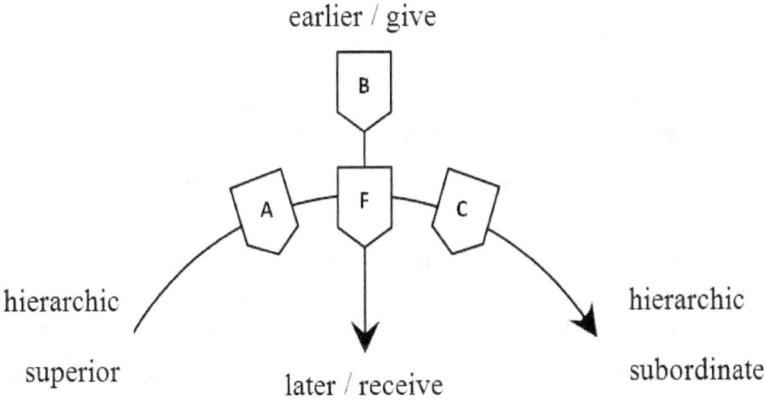

Graph. 4: *Typical possible interpretations of the positions of representatives.*

Position relative to F	Relation of F to functional units	Relation of F to values and resources
A on the right	A is hierarchic superior	A is an orientation-creating value or a resource to develop
B behind	-	B is an integrated value or an internal resource
C on the left	C is subordinate	C is a resource that is effectively used

Table 2: Possible ways of reading the positions (according to the directions of Bert Hellinger, Gunthard Weber, Varga von Kibéd and I. Sparrer 2000, p. 171 ff)

5.6 Interventions

The facilitator always tries to use his interventions to open up possible courses of action for his clients. He has the following options:

• to explain the effect of (relational) structures by questioning the representatives.

• to change the constellation to allow as many representatives as possible to improve their relationship with the system as a whole. If required, he can introduce representatives for new elements and have them put in position.

• to prompt the representatives to follow their motion impulses and to try out new positions.

• to test and simulate alternatives, in order to learn relevant differences.

Depending on the experience and working style of the facilitator these interventions have different outcomes. Instead of a comprehensive description of all possibilities, we offer some hints at this point that have been proven in practice.

As a rule in a business context, it makes sense to begin by changing the position of the "focus". This is in accordance with the fact that also in reality the client has to make the first move to bring about a change. In order to stress the fact that the responsibility for implementing the findings of the constellation lies with the client the "focus" can be asked which move should be tried out first. Team members, who are not positioned in the constellation, can also make suggestions for such a move.

An important intervention serves to separate confounded or confused elements. In the case of a suspected overlapping of an element with "extraneous" aspects, the facilitator can hold his hand behind or in front of the representative's face and then gradually move it aside. If the relationship of the "focus" and the other representative improves, then this is an indication that there was overlapping. Then a new representative is selected and positioned to represent the overlapping element.

This technique, known as "work with the cataleptic hand" (Insa Sparrer und Matthias Varga von Kibéd), is especially suitable for tests or also when there are not enough people to be representatives. If the facilitator suspects that an important element of the constellation is missing, he can test this by holding the cataleptic hand over the appropriate spot.

In the case of representatives who for inexplicable reasons do not relate well to each other, it is helpful to have them change places for a moment so that they can see the situation from the other's point of view.

The so-called restitution ritual is a form of context separation in which a liability that has been assumed by a person not responsible for it, is restored in a symbolic way. The "encumbered" representative is given a heavy object which he then gives back to that representative to whom the liability can be traced back. In this way e.g. the successor company of a failed company could hand back the responsibility for the failure to the original company if evidence surfaces in the constellation that the managers of the new company bear a burden that it is not theirs.

5.7 Conclusion

It is up to the facilitator to decide when to close the constellation and discuss the insights gained. The constellation is regarded as closed as soon as a satisfactory answer or alternative solution has been found. Usually the initial image already offers an abundance of information. The first moves that lead the system out of an impasse are the most important.

We have had positive experience marking the final image with place markers for the representatives and afterwards offering all team members the chance to try out various positions and experience the solution from different points of view.

We have pointed out on various occasions that, after a constellation, the impressions from the constellation should be exchanged and are expanded further in a dialogue or discussion. In any event, we think that such a change in language is advisable. This way the impressions are transferred from the "perceptive" level to the linguistic level. At the same time, the individual reflections intensify into a meaningful co-creative whole. A common focus develops. The facilitator participates actively in the dialogue and thus brings his experience to bear when "reading" the constellation.

Against this background those measures that prove themselves to be helpful and useful in firming-up a solution in the organization are identified. This happens in small groups in the setting of a traditional workshop sequence moderated by the facilitator or in a large group for example, with a World Café (Juanita Brown) or Open Space (Harrison Owen). We go into more detail with the last-mentioned intervention practice in chapter 7.

CHAPTER 6

SELECTED MENTAL MODELS AND CORRESPONDING CONSTELLATION FORMATS

As we have already seen, setting up a constellation is always preceded by choosing the system segment to be investigated as well as the perspective from which it is viewed. In doing so, a mental model guides the searching process. It is a kind of map that sets out the boundaries and highlights certain features, or rather elements that are important for solving the problem.

In addition, a mental model serves as a kind of navigator during the constellation process and makes focussing on the selected segment of the system easier. Furthermore, a mental model can offer guidance when developing measures based on the constellation.

Each facilitator takes a mental model as a basis, even if not always consciously, for his decision on what is to be set up or not. Based on his repertoire of theories and experience he chooses a set of interconnected variables that appear to fit the situation being explored.

According to our experience, it is important in a management context that the facilitator is aware of his underlying assumptions and can also make these clear if required. These form the background of the understanding between facilitator and manager, when they interpret the constellation and decide the options for action. The managers should be able to understand the selected mental model, but in order to produce new solutions, it should also encourage new points of view.

As a constellation format, we indicate the way a certain mental model can be staged. A format determines the elements to be set up and in some cases also how to proceed with the constellation. The following pages offer a selection of such mental models together with the relevant constellation formats. They have all proven themselves in practice.

At this point we would like to mention an observation we have made in the workshops and peer supervision groups. Some facilitators cling too closely to certain formats. We therefore invite our readers to take a flexible approach. It is better for problem solving to trust one's own intuition and to follow the course of events rather than cling desperately to a model.

To afford a better overview, we have arranged the models and formats under three main headings:

- Management and leadership,
- Strategy and innovation,
- Problem solving and decision making.

In order to offer an insight into the various techniques used in actual constellation work, we describe situations from our intervention practice with varying attention to detail. However, it is also valid here that the technique is not the main priority. Becoming involved in what makes the constellation resonate is. For this reason, it is important for a facilitator to take care that the representatives maintain their presence and focus their attention on physical sensations as well as on the changes taking place in their surroundings. They should not start discussing their experience prematurely. A moment of peace is central to the constellation process. The really innovative and sustainable solutions are the result of peace and quiet.

6.1 Management and Leadership

The interaction between the various functional units (departments, teams, executive committees, business divisions etc.), with reference to a specific objective, concerns a large number of management topics. For this range of topics, we present four models with the associated formats that respectively bring a specific aspect of the organizational action to the fore.

Whenever you use a model, you will be reminded that a system constellation (as with any other research) always only deals with a very specific cross section of an organization. Accordingly, it never comprises the whole organization. The result of a constellation therefore does not constitute "the all-embracing truth"; it is the basis for hypotheses which contribute to develop the necessary interventions.

In this way a constellation can indeed change the picture that a manager makes of an actual situation. Maybe his approach to this actual situation changes at the same time, but a constellation on its own will not change the situation itself. The dynamics which emerge in a system constellation must be carried out by the managers themselves in their actual organizations as concrete measures for shaping, developing and managing their business. A facilitator should always point out that:

Constellation work does not replace action! It "only" indicates the rules and principles on which this action should be based and indicates the direction for action.

6.1.1 St. Gallen Management Model

The St. Gallen management model supplies a sophisticated and coherent description of the interplay between the structuring factors of an organization. In addition, it shows the interconnections between these structuring factors and the routines in various processes (Graph. 5).

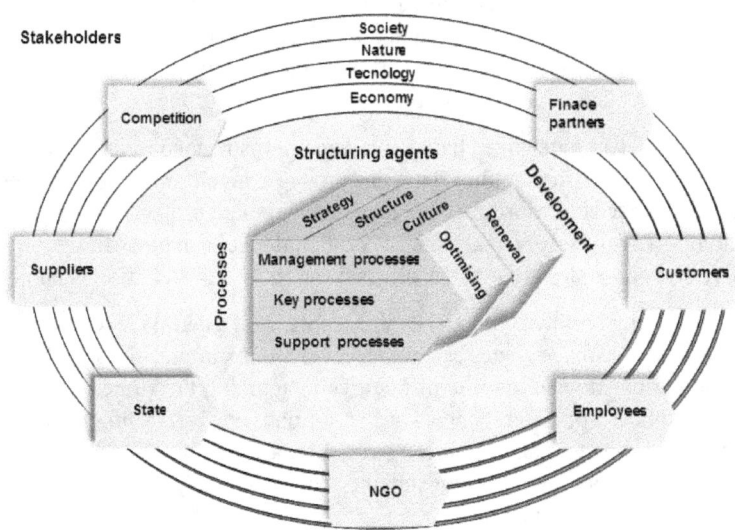

Graph. 5: St. Gallen Management Model

In addition, the model names the relevant players or stakeholders of a company: its employees, customers, suppliers and financial backers. Depending on the topic further differentiations are possible and sensible within these groups, for example, splitting employees between managers and office staff or between sales and production or between employees working on projects and those in line functions, etc.

The model distinguishes various process levels in a further dimension such as management, business and support processes. Following this model, the facilitator can focus on the relationship between the players and their specific tasks. In this way the constellation gives a precise picture of the dynamics between the groups of people involved. If a job is substantiated as "product development" or "order processing" - and is not left unspecified under the title of "task" – the parties involved are easier to spot and, if need be, represented in the constellation.

In addition, the St. Gallen Model distinguishes between activities that preserve the system and those that change it; this is then especially useful if issues relating to projects have to be resolved. Therefore it is advisable in the case of project constellations to add a representative for the processes that maintain the status quo.

The answers gained in the constellation can be classified with the help of this model into a normative, strategic and operational level and thus draw conclusions about the consequences of a certain solution. This makes it possible to introduce the planned measures at the right level and scope.

For example, less extensive change management is needed to implement solutions at an operational rather than on a strategic level. As a rule, a strategic realignment needs a co-ordinated change management project with the corresponding structures. Reversals at an operational level can be dealt with more easily; often an insight that materializes through the constellation is enough.

As constellations show again and again, problems at a certain level have their roots in the unresolved issues at a higher level. For example, in a specific case a constellation showed that the difficulties in agreeing the strategy development were based on discrepancies at the normative level. Conflicts between the board of directors and the management regarding corporate governance, the basic values and the mission statement had obviously impeded the company's clear, strategic positioning.

The St. Gallen Model is well suited as a basis for the specific format known as "organization constellation". As a rule this format is used to answer the following questions:

• How do the functions relate to the objective or task?

Selected mental models and corresponding constellation formats

- How is control distributed among the functions?
- Where are there possible conflicts among the functions?
- Which functions are excluded?
- How are the operational functions supported by management or support functions?

The following are the standard elements for this format:

- A job or task with a corresponding objective,
- Formally commissioned or rather involved functions and players at various levels,
- Other concerned or involved stakeholders,
- Relevant context factors such as e.g., strategy or certain values.

Sketching the organogram on a flip chart can help to determine the elements to be set up. When using this format care should be taken not to draw attention to the personal aspects of the relationship between the jobholders, but to the structural aspects of the relationship between the functions.

An example of this: The head of the dental technology division of a large manufacturer complained about resistance to implementing the new strategy. A resolution was sought at a workshop with the divisional manager, his executive team and the person responsible for organization and human resources development. They decided to set up an organization constellation. Fig. 4 shows the initial situation.

96 Enacting solutions

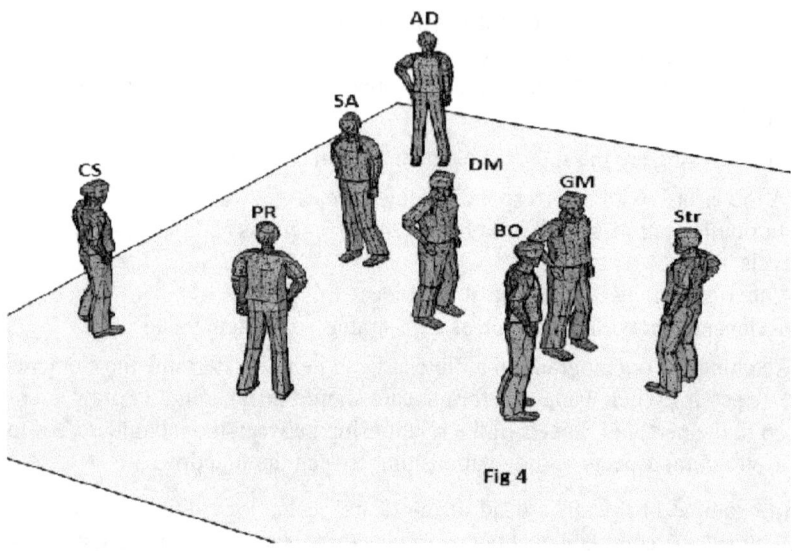

Fig. 4: Implementation of a new strategy – original image

Str Strategy
SA Sales
BO Board of directors
CS Customer service

GM General Manager
AD Administration
DM Divisional manager
PR Production

The *divisional manager* depends on the *general manager* who has developed the new strategy and wants to implement it. In doing so, the *divisional manager* loses sight of what is currently happening in his own line of business. *Sales and distribution* is embroiled in a dispute with *customer service* and *production* is waiting with growing irritation for the *divisional manager* to concern himself finally with their serious operational problems. The *administration* distances itself from everything and adopts a wait and see attitude. The *divisional manager's* dilemma is very clear: how can he comply with the demands of the *general manager* and at the same time support his employees?

The first move of the divisional manager, difficult though it was, consisted in positioning himself to the left of strategy which implies at the same time being at its service. This also prompted the *board of directors, customer service* and *production* to align themselves to a common objective. Fig. 5 reproduces the result.

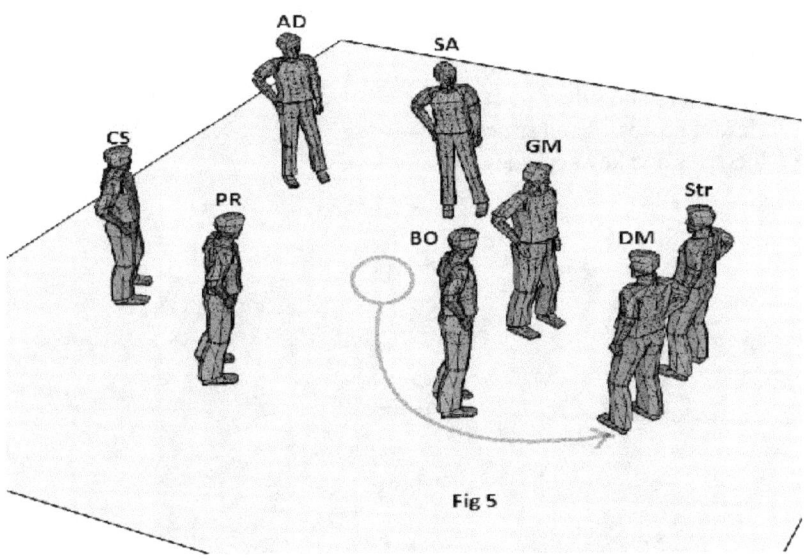

Fig. 5: Implementation of a new strategy – final chart

Str Strategy
PR Production
BO Board of directors
SA Sales

GM General Manager
CU Customer service
DM Divisional manager
AD Administration

The result was that the *divisional manager* succeeded in raising for the first time all concerns about the new strategy with the *general manager* and the *board of directors*. They agreed to deal with this topic in a workshop at first management level. In this way, the *divisional manager* gained the respect of his employees and could involve them in a constructive discussion on the gradual implementation of the strategy.

6.1.2 Epidauros Model

Our consultancy showed us that frequently participants did not really take the trouble to understand the other person's point of view. This was most

likely because the business partners started out with different assumptions that they did not clarify with each other. These tacit assumptions are to be found mostly at the following logical levels (Graph. 6):
- Narrative and analysis of the history of development,
- Definition of the system and its environment,
- Raison d'être of the company,
- Basic values and rules,
- Relevant processes and structures,
- Objectives and key activities.

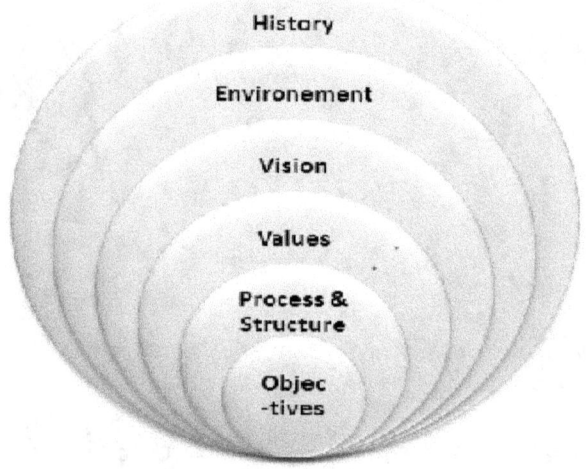

Graph. 6: Epidauros Model

It has been proven time and again that it is useful to explore and share these tacit assumptions in a shorter or longer process. Generally in doing so resources can appear that play an important role for problem-solving. The following keywords and questions on the various levels help a team to discuss the implicit propositions and to correct any likely misunderstandings. They also serve to highlight any gaps that can then be closed off later.

History

Intention: To recognise and appreciate the achievements of various people; to recognise behavior patterns and to note their effect; to sum up important phases of the development hitherto.

Questions: What steps have brought us here? What were the common and private experiences? What are our sources and roots?

System/environment

Intention: To identify the relevant in-house and external players;

to define the limits of the system; to identify the general conditions and fields of action.

Questions: Who is part of the system? Are the limits clear? What is the origin of our resources? What are the legal, social and financial basic requirements? With whom are we in contact? Who are our customers and suppliers?

Vision

Intention: To create a common picture for the future; to identify diverse ideas and co-ordinate them.

Questions: What do we want to achieve and contribute? How are the ideas of individuals integrated together? How does our vision appear from the perspective of various stakeholders? From what do we create motivation and power?

Values

Intention: To develop rules as a guideline for action.

Questions: By what behavior, attitudes and results will we be recognized? What are the values, rules and limits that constitute our identity?

Business processes and structure

Intention: To define and distribute the tasks; to design organizational and process structures; to agree procedures for decisions and actions.

Questions: What are the essential processes for realizing our vision? What structures are needed to manage these processes? Which tasks are delegated to which person and board? Is the structure suitable for implementing our values and vision?

Objectives and key activities

Intention: To plan implementation steps and feedback loops; to determine priorities.

Questions: Which activities are needed? In what order? How will the results become apparent?

6.1.3 Applying the Epidauros Model

One aspect of the model is that it is a useful map to clarify key topics at the beginning of a larger process. It integrates all levels that are important for the development, design and control of a system. Another one is to suggest a coherent series of clarification steps. For instance, before a vision can be approved, it would be useful to make a topic of disruptions in the history.

Ideally the model is used in a constellation for diagnostic purposes. The focus (company management, project team) is set up with a representative for each of the six levels of the model. This constellation shows which level has the unsolved questions. These can be dealt with in a further specific constellation or with other methods.

Fig. 6 shows a constellation with a team of the training department of an entrepreneurs association. The working atmosphere had deteriorated; the employees felt that they were overworked. The manager of the department wanted to optimize working procedures further. However the consultant was able to convince him to begin with an Epidauros workshop to ascertain where the problem lay.

Selected mental models and corresponding constellation formats 101

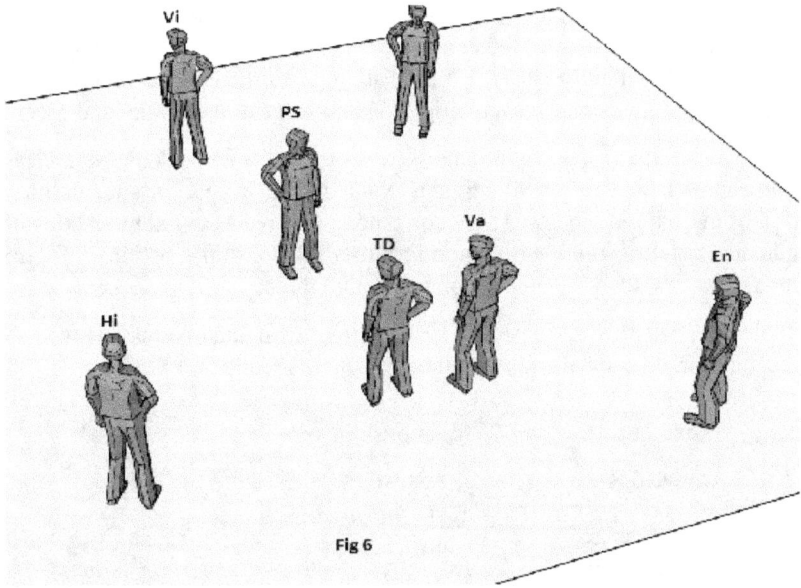

Fig. 6: working atmosphere in further education department

TD Training department
Va values
Hi History
PS Processes/structures

En Environment
Ob Objectives
Vi Vision

As the constellation made clear, the team became so focussed on adhering to the internal processes that it had lost sight and touch of the current situation, i.e., with the members of the entrepreneurs association and what they expected from the training. As a result, it was no longer appreciated by the outsiders. This ultimately was the decisive reason for the lack of motivation.

The question for resolving the problem therefore was not: "How can we arrange our work routines more efficiently?", but "How can we establish again a constructive dialogue with the members of the association?"

6.1.4 Values and resources triangle

The values and resources triangle is a useful model to use whenever it is a matter of exploring which resources are to be activated and used in a situation, or rather, which values determine the precise behavior in a team or organization. It reverts back to the concept of "belief polarities" as developed by Varga von Kibéd and Sparrer, which distinguishes three basic values found in differing dimensions in each religion: knowledge, trust or faith and order.

These three aspects can capture the system of values of a person or organization comprehensively: each individual value results from a certain combination of these three aspects. These correspond to three essential modalities of human existence: thinking – entering into a relationship – action. A fourth modality – "wisdom" – incorporates the other three.

Table 3 shows how the aspects "knowledge", "trust" and "order" as well as the appropriate concepts fall into the three first modalities.

Thinking	Relationship	Action
Knowledge	**Trust**	**Order**
logic, knowledge, intuition, curiosity, experience, clarity, vision, comprehension, ...	aesthetics, openness, loyalty, respect, empathy, esteem, ...	ethics, reliability, duty, hierarchy, fairness, functionality, balance, ...

Tab. 3: Value polarities (according to Varga von Kibéd and Sparrer)

Below we describe, by way of example, two application possibilities.

Sample application 1

This example was all about checking which values are followed by a team in a certain situation and how they could change in the course of a development project.

Three pin boards were set up in the room to form an equilateral triangle that offered enough space for team members to move freely. Each pin board represented one of the basic values: knowledge, trust or order. To begin with, team members noted on the pin boards those values that they would actively experience in the company, or rather, team. In this way, a coordinate system emerged that expressed the business culture. The team members could then take their personal position in this coordinate system by placing themselves at the appropriate spot in the room.

Selected mental models and corresponding constellation formats

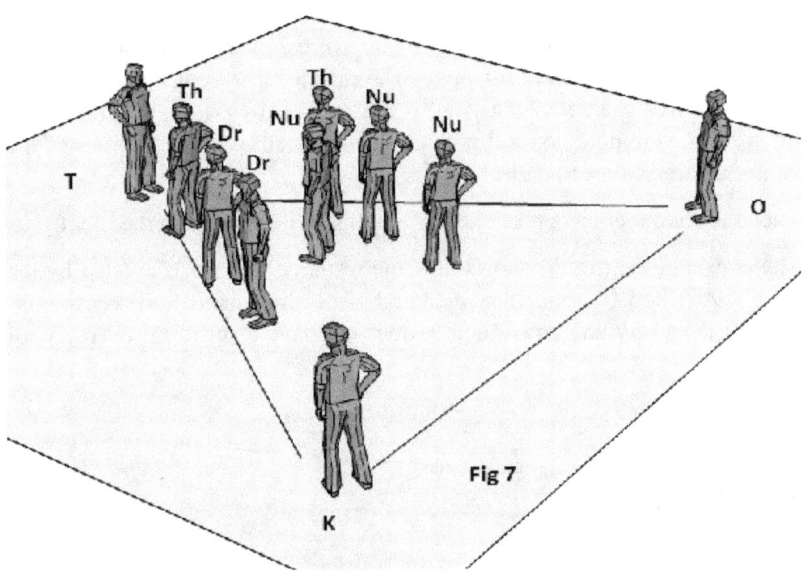

Fig. 7: Diagnosis at the beginning of a workshop

T Trust
O Order
K Knowledge

Nu Nurses
Drs Doctors
Th Therapists

Fig. 7 shows how the members of the working group of a hospital were positioned: All team members position themselves mainly towards the value trust. The values, knowledge and order have proportionately little weight. This gave valuable indications for the design of the development process by concentrating first of all on the question: "Which rules and structures have we to agree so that we can work together well as a team?"

A possible development is checked out in a second move by asking team members to turn their attention to another combination of values and move to a new position to find out how it has affected them and the whole team.

This constellation had several positive effects: firstly, the team members would be aware which position they represent in the team in respect of basic values. Secondly, an overall visible and tangible picture of the prevailing team culture appeared. Thirdly, an idea about the direction in which the team would be able to develop emerged.

Sample application 2

Here it was a matter of empowering a team to cross over from a conflict-laden discussion to a productive dialogue. The managers were asked to describe which features characterise a good result of the discussion. The keywords referred to were noted on a flip chart and assigned to the modalities of the values and resources triangle.

Then the team members placed the following five elements in the room:

The constellation (fig. 8) shows how the resource of *trust* is averted by the *team*. *Order* and *knowledge* have a good place, the *team* is however too fixated on the *result* and consequently does not have a sufficient overview of the *resources*.

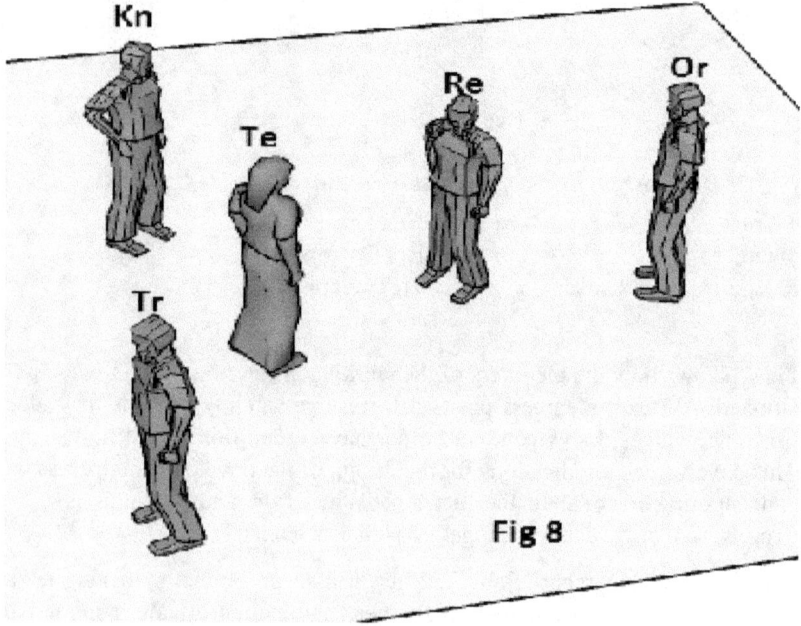

Fig. 8: Productive dialogue – first phase

Te Team   Or Order
Re Result   Kn Knowledge
Tr Trust

After the representatives had moved freely and sought a better place, the result was the constellation as shown in fig. 9: there was now a good contact with all three resources. *Trust* "protects" the *team's* way to the *result*. As a result of the insights gained from the system constellation, the conversation was now productive and without any friction.

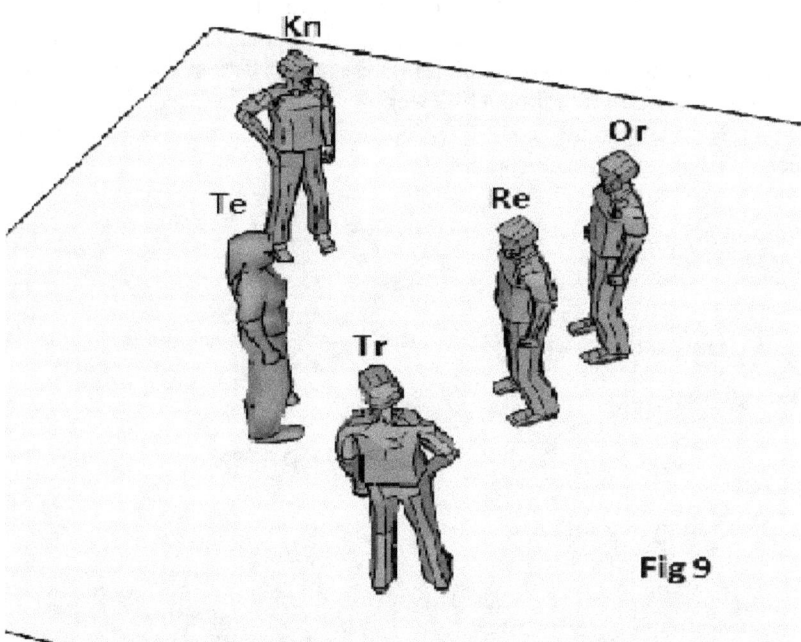

Fig. 9: Productive dialogue – closing image

Te Team
Tr Trust
Re Result

Kn Knowledge
Or Order

6.1.5 TCI Model

It often makes sense, especially when analyzing and processing the dynamics of a team, not to pay attention to the relationships of the team members to each other, but instead to the relationship of the team to its task, leader, and context in which the team should work and the overriding raison d'être of the task. A constellation format based on the TCI model by Ruth Cohn (Cohn 1975) is suitable for this.

TCI stands for "Theme centred interaction". The model includes the following four factors: I (individual) – us (group) – it (theme) – globe (environment). For the purposes of this study, we have specified these four elements as follows – leader, team, task, context – and complemented them by a further element: raison d'être (Graph. 7). These factors determine decisively the capacity for work. In a productive working situation the leader has his eye on the team as well as the task. The context as well as the raison d'être are perceived as supporting resources.

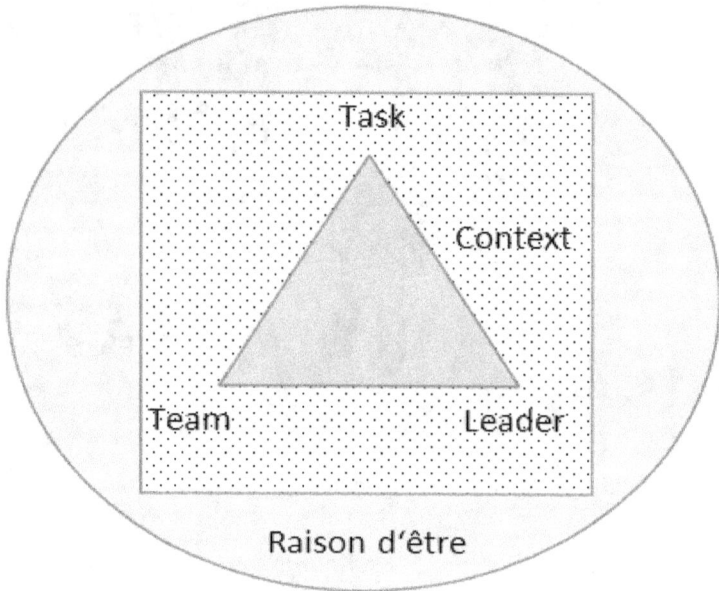

Graph. 7: A modified TCI model for the constellation in management contexts

Sample application

The constellation shows the situation in the product development department of a medium-sized manufacturer (fig. 10).

Selected mental models and corresponding constellation formats 107

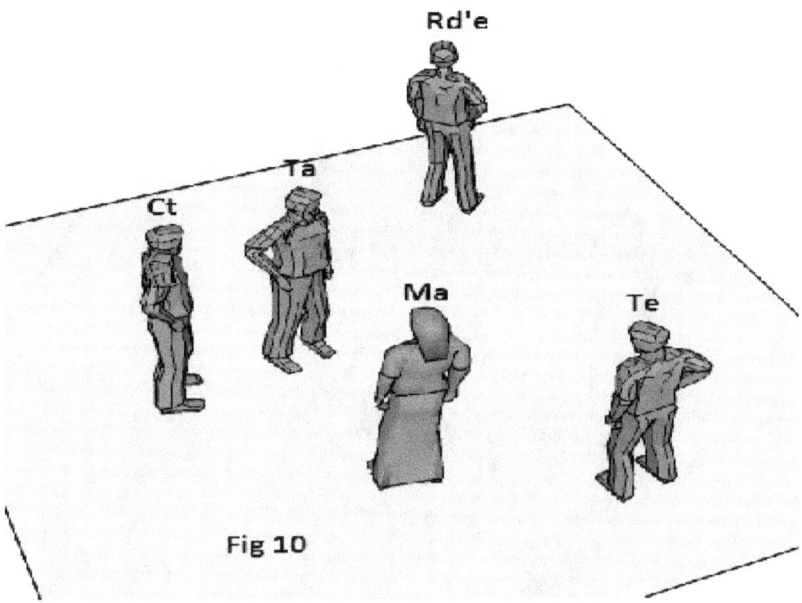

Fig. 10: Situation in a management team

Te Team   Rd'e Raison d'être
Co Context   Ma Manager
Ta Task

In answer to the question about possible sources of irritation, it transpired that the departmental manager had only been with the company for a few months and that his predecessor had left after an argument with the CEO about the strategic direction of product development. The strategic direction had not been discussed with the team members. This explains why the *raison d'être* is positioned so far away in the constellation.

The first step towards a solution consisted of the *context* approaching the *raison d'être* (fig. 11).

108   *Enacting solutions*

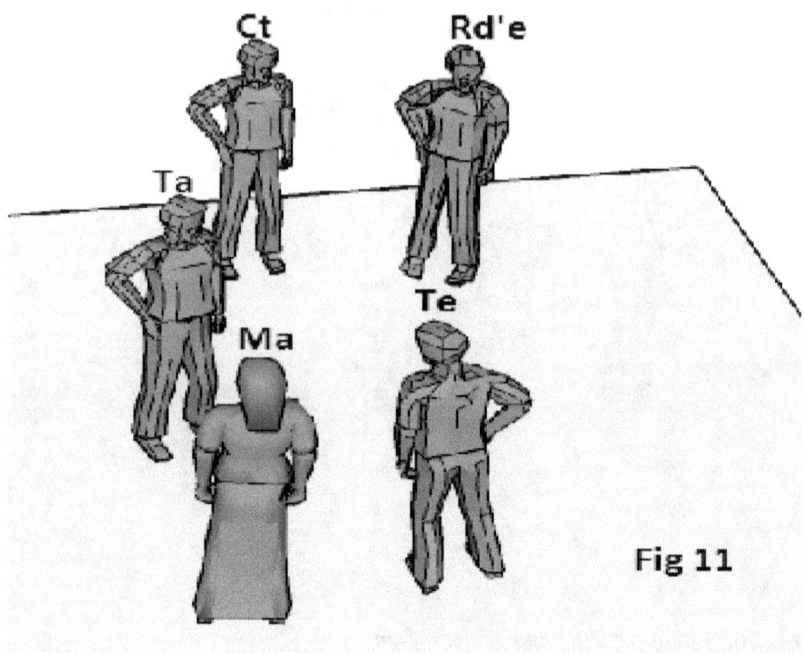

Fig. 11 Situation in a management team – development

Te Team   Co Context
Ta Task   Rd'e Raison d'être
Le Manager

Only now could the *team* and *leader* draw nearer to each other and the *team* could concentrate on the *task*.

The constellation gave the managers the incentive to finally address the background of the change of management and the controversies in the strategic direction.

6.2 Strategy and Innovation

A whole series of models and concepts are available for this topic which deals with the validation and development of strategic options. We have decided to present the following four models because, on the one hand, they cover a

wide range of applications and, on the other, because they are very different from each other:
- Strategy Maps,
- Butterfly model,
- Values square and
- Development of potential.

6.2.1 Strategy Maps

The strategy maps (Kaplan and Norton 2004) that have been developed by Robert S. Kaplan and David P. Norton on the basis of the "balanced scorecard" is a model that is accepted and applied worldwide. Both authors identify four perspectives from which a company can be surveyed:

- **Financial perspective:** describes the tangible results of the strategy according to typical business-management parameters.

- **Customer perspective:** defines the value proposition for target customers, as it is incorporated in a marketing mix for example.

- **Internal process perspective:** includes the value creation processes by which customer value is generated.

- **Learning and development perspective:** identifies the immaterial capital or potential that are important for implementing the strategy.

The different aspects of this model offer a comprehensive pattern that helps to locate the relevant factors in a specific situation. An important aspect of this model is the interdependence of the four perspectives (graph. 8). For instance, the financial objectives can only be achieved if the company develops something of value for which customers are prepared to pay a price. This, for its part, is generated by aligned, functional processes. The latter are related together with the so-called immaterial resources: human, information and organization capital.

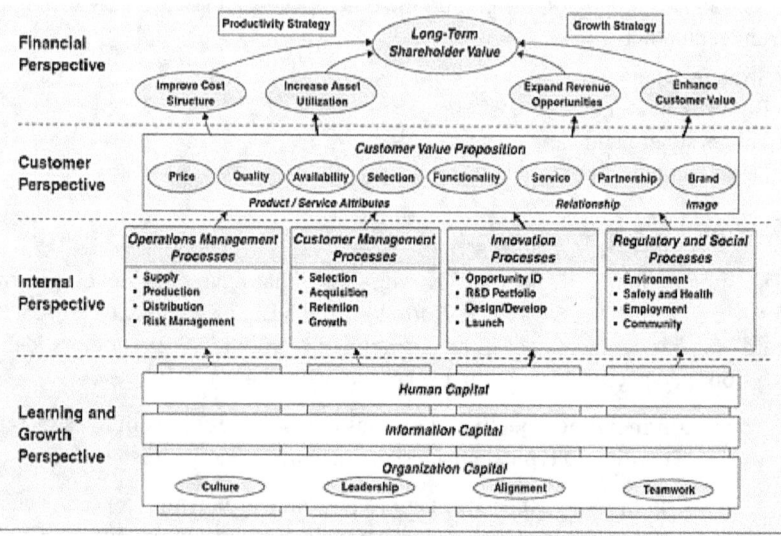

Graph. 8: Strategy Map (modified according to Kaplan and Norton 2004) (RO-NOA = Return on Net Operating Assets)

Especially in the case of strategic problems, strategy maps offer, as their name indicates, a good orientation for the definition of a system segment and scope as well as of the elements to be set up.

If for example we want to examine the consistency of a strategy of product leadership with the help of the system constellation, then representatives for the quality of products, new customer segments, innovation process, expertise and creativity cannot be lacking.

6.2.2 Butterfly model

Projects need different resources in their various phases, from their conception to their implementation. Therefore it is sensible to examine the project portfolio repeatedly to find out what the projects need in each current phase and, at the same time, who has to take on which role. Henriette Lingg (Rosselet, Senoner and Lingg 2007, p. 161 ff) has developed a model for dealing with such questions that includes the following components:

- Egg – symbolizes the phase of developing the idea.

- Caterpillar – stands for the phase of gathering information and resources.
- Chrysalis – means the phase of transformation, the project is taking on its precise shape.
- Butterfly – symbolizes the result, the realization, but also the transience of the idea.

We illustrate the constellation format again with an example. A leading civil servant, who was supposed to draw up a draft bill on promoting innovation, wanted to identify the reasons for the difficulties in finding a consensus between the various parties involved. In a work group of employees of the department and politicians, the consultants carried out a constellation with the aid of a butterfly model. The representatives of the different players involved in the process placed themselves intuitively in a grid marked on the floor with the four fields of egg – caterpillar – chrysalis – butterfly (Fig. 12).

The constellation speaks volumes: politicians and the trade unions were busy dealing with basic ideological questions; employers were looking at the situation from a great distance and wanted more information; the public took their place behind the officials and were not very interested in the law; the civil servants were completely focussed on the draft bill; the only ones, who also focussed on the law, were the research institutes, who according to the draft bill should play an important role in the innovation process; the media were only interested in the public and already considered the law to be a failure.

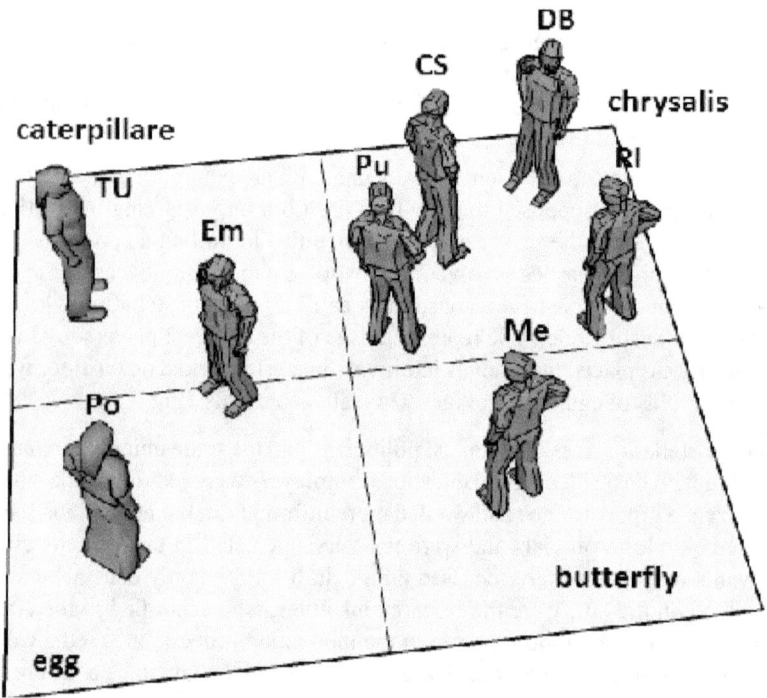

Fig. 12: Developing a draft bill – first phase

DB Draft bill
Pu Members of the public
Po Politics
CS Civil servants

TU Trade union
RI Research institutes
Em Employers
Me Media

The representatives were asked to simulate the next sensible step in developing the draft bill and to take up an appropriate place in the four fields (Fig. 13) The *draft bill* went "back" into the caterpillar field: "Even more information, especially about the situation and the needs of the employers, has to be gathered."

The *civil servant* turned round and was able to have a dialogue now with his most important interlocutors, *employers* and *research institutes*.

The *research institutes* took their place on the border between the butterfly and the egg: "On the one hand, I have a clear idea about how *employers* and

Selected mental models and corresponding constellation formats 113

research institutes should work together ideally; on the other hand, it is perhaps not yet time to implement these."

The *employers* kept their distance, but were interested in speaking to the *civil servant*.

The *politicians* withdrew a little from the confrontation with the *trade unions* who remained focussed on the *politicians*.

The *public* withdrew from the centre.

The *media* continued to show no real interest in the *draft bill*.

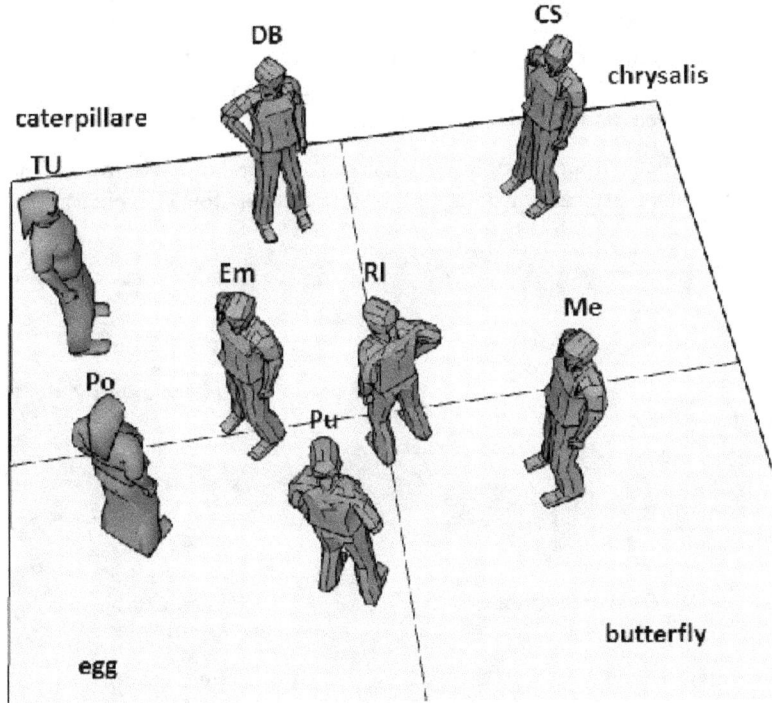

Fig. 13: Developing a draft bill – follow-up chart

DB Draft bill
Pu Public
Pol Politicians
Em Employers

RI Research institutes
TU Trade union
CS Civil servant

The working group was able to get valuable insights from this constellation for the next steps and the law was passed a few months later.

A variant of the butterfly format consists of the four development steps not marked as fields in the room, but carried out by representatives. The metaphor of the butterfly has the advantage that it is very perspicuous and demonstrates the development steps of the project convincingly.

6.2.3 Square of values

Values are an important part of business culture. They determine the limits of employee behavior. Usually it is assumed that everyone knows the values according to which they have to act. However, Friedemann Schulz von Thun's (Schulz von Thun 1989) model shows that values are only meaningful if their overstatement and complementary value are seen in context.

With the help of an example we want to illustrate how Schulz von Thun's model can be used as a pattern for a system constellation (Graph. 9).

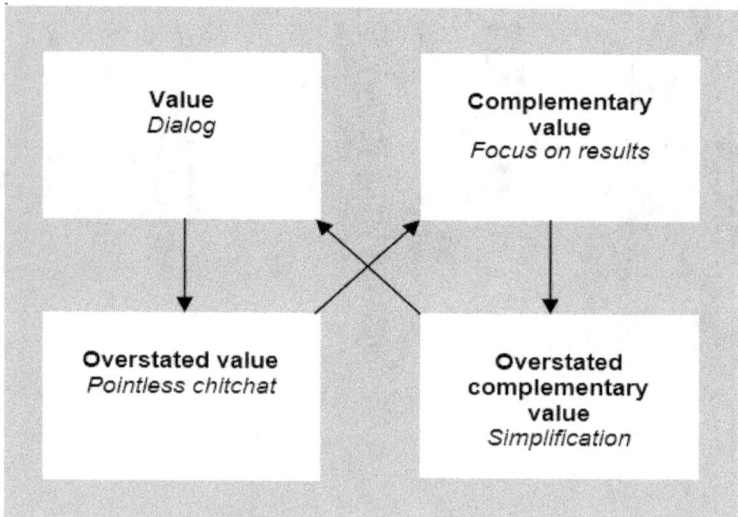

Graph. 9: Square of values

The team of the human resources department of a public transport company had developed a new concept for training their staff, but met with little understanding and approval from the top management.

Selected mental models and corresponding constellation formats 115

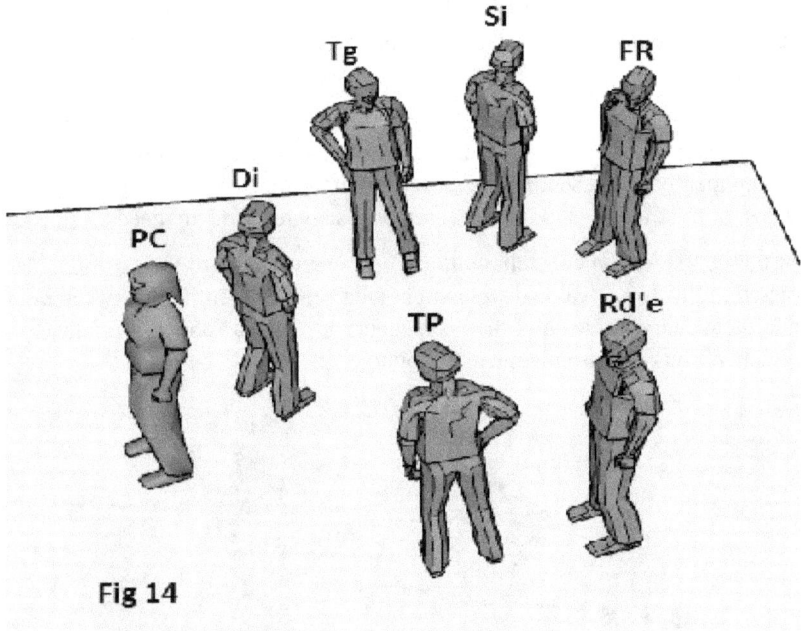

Fig 14

Fig. 14: Acceptance of a training plan - starting image

TP Training plan
FR Focussing on results
Tg Target group

Si simplification
Di Dialogue
Rd'e Raison d'être
PC pointless chitchat

The consultants posed the question: "What is the essential new value on which the concept is based and in which ways is it different from the values hitherto effective?"

Training should be aimed much more intensely on dialogue between the participants to work out solutions together and less on passing on technical knowledge by traditional classroom teaching. For this reason *dialogue* was chosen as the designation for this new central value. When exaggerated it is described as *pointless chitchat* and its complementary value as *focussing on results* and when overemphasized it is described as *simplification*.

Fig. 14 shows how the team members depicted the situation. Several aspects in the starting image of this constellation stand out: the possibility to exaggerate the dialogue with *pointless chitchat* is not envisaged; *focussing on results* and *simplification* are experienced as opposites, between which there is no compromise; the *raison d'être* is fixed solely on the *training plan.*

As a representative for the *raison d'être* the manageress of the personnel department sums it up aptly: "I feel that I am the sole purpose of the plan", and a team member representing the *target group* thinks: "I expect that the *raison d'être* of the training should be geared primarily towards my needs."

In the course of the constellation, the managers moved to the positions depicted in fig. 15: a "value development area" can be identified between both complementary values and their exaggerations, i.e., a room materializes in which various compromises can be found.

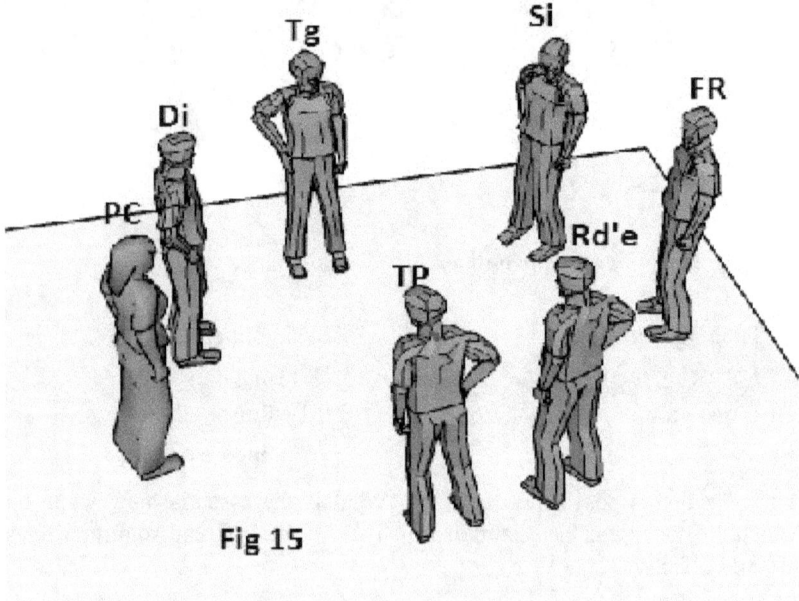

Fig. 15: Acceptance of a training plan - development

TP Training plan
FR Focussing on results
Tg Target group
PC pointless chitchat

Si simplification
Di Dialogue
Rd'e Raison d'être

The constellation has shown the team members how they had disregarded the values and ideas of their target group by concentrating on their new concept and that consequently their plan could be neither understood nor accepted by their target group.

6.2.4 Development of potential

A constellation format, which can be used to investigate how to develop the potential of a team or a company, follows the "autopoietic constellation" developed by Siegfried Essen, an approach which expresses the self organization of living systems by very specific interventions that are guided by the following principles (Essen 2003, p. 34):

- The system is complete. It needs nothing from outside and no element is superfluous.
- The meaning of the various parts of the system originates in action.
- There is no end to development. There are only temporary solutions.

The basic elements of our format derived from this are:

- The company in its current shape and form,
- The strategic objectives of the company,
- The company's potential for development,
- Various context factors depending on the specific issue.

The design of the constellation process is what is special about this format. The representatives take their places in the room in order to depict the current situation and then move about in slow motion, in response to the various impulses they feel, in order to find a good place within the whole system. The facilitator keeps stalling the process and asking the representatives to express their experience in words. This format is suitable for resolving dysfunctional patterns of thought and makes space for unexpected options for development.

As we have noticed repeatedly, managers tend to overlook some of the factors which determine the development of their company. For example, the senior management of a company that had been taken over by an international group of companies was able to recognise in a constellation that they had hitherto not occupied themselves with the question of what new potential they were capable of developing within the new context of the group. Instead they had focussed exclusively on the objective of securing their current market position and the continuity of their manufacturing base.

6.3 Problem solving and decision making

These kinds of topics deal with finding ways out of deadlock situations or dead ends and putting a stop to a dysfunctional pattern of interaction. Conflicts and logjams often occur if important aspects are suppressed, mixed or confused.

6.3.1 Tetralemma

The Tetralemma is a model that goes back to traditional Indian logic (Varga von Kibed and Sparrer 2000, p. 77). It is useful for overcoming blockages. When challenged to take a decision, the question keeps coming up about which alternative is the "right one". Is it one or the other? Would chances be better with a combination of options that only apparently exclude each other? Or does success lie beyond the possibilities discussed?

The name Tetralemma implies four positions in contrast to dilemma that implies only two:

1. The position of "the one".
2. Its opposite is the "the other".
3. The position "both" that points to the hitherto overseen compatibility of the former positions. *Both* can mean for example:
   - there is a compromise and either *one* or *both* can be effective,
   - to incorporate the quality of the non-chosen alternative into the one chosen,
   - the contrasts are only apparent as such,
   - an unexpected combination of *one* with the *other* to produce a new alternative.
4. The position of *neither of them* denotes the context in which the original contrast makes sense. It can for instance point out that it is about something else, that an important aspect was suppressed, that the contrast has occurred in a very specific context and has lost importance in another context.

   Matthias Varga von Kibed and Insa Sparrer supplement the model with a fifth position:

5. The position *Not all this - and not even that* has "the peculiarity of breaking the pattern time and again" (ibid., p. 89 f). It means wisdom or creativity and is also called "a free element" and indicates a completely unexpected solution on another logical level.

Varga von Kibed and Sparrer describe several possibilities for applying the model as a constellation format. With the "traditional version", the representatives of the first four positions are placed in a circle looking inwards and so that they form the corners of a square. The fifth position, after it has been set up, is allowed to move freely in the room. The facilitator guides the person representing the client (often denominated as "focus") from one to all other positions, placing him first on the left and then on the right side of the respective position. After each re-setting, the differences are noted. For this reason, the Tetralemma is described as "a landscape that changes as we cross it and because we are doing that" (ibid., p. 86).

The free form of the tetralemma format is also suitable for applying in management contexts. The five positions and the "focus" are placed freely in the room in agreement with the inner image of the managers. This makes clear for the most part which options were suppressed. Their inclusion makes the way clear for new insights.

Example of use

The following example comes from a process of developing a mission statement in a large planning office. The participants had already formulated several principles when a fierce discussion broke out on the subject "Responsibility for the environment". They referred to a specific project they had been commissioned. Some employees suspected that the customer was speculating at the expense of the environment. "How honest are we really," an engineer asked, "if we declare to commit ourselves to the environment and then accept a contract like this?" We suggested dealing with the dilemma, whether or not to accept or refuse this contract, with the help of a tetralemma constellation.

The result of the constellation was baffling (fig. 16). The representatives had hardly taken their positions when the representative of the *office* said: "We cannot refuse this project." Also the representative of the alternative *to refuse* said: "I have chosen this role because I have always taken the position that we should not accept this project. As I am however personally in this role, it is clear to me that it would be wrong to refuse it." The representative of *neither of them* said: "If the local authority has approved the project, we, as the planning office, are not authorised to reject it." The representative for *both* added: "We can demonstrate our environmental awareness by suggesting alternatives within the scope of the approved project to the builders that would best protect the environment".

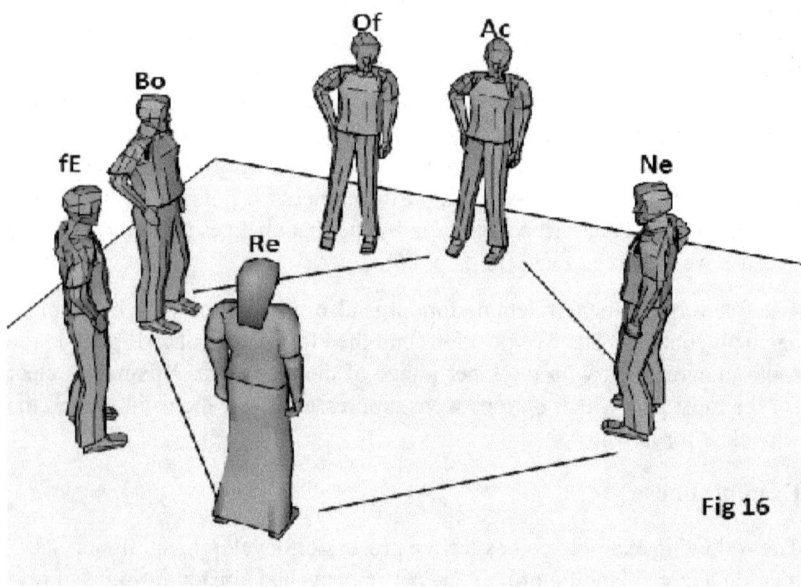

Fig. 16: Critical decision

Of Office
Bo Both
Ac Accept

Ne Neither of them
Re Reject
fE free element: "None of this and not even that"

As all positions are represented at the same time in the room and are seen as a whole, what is hardly possible in a discussion comes easier with decision making. Sometimes you even have the feeling that the result emerges on its own.

6.3.2 Structure of a problem

Each problem has an objective that has to be achieved and obstacles that stand in the way of achieving the objective. The obstacles can be overcome only if there are appropriate resources available.

The interaction of obstacle and resource is an important aspect that can be worked on in a system constellation. Obstacles can suddenly reveal themselves as potential resources. Indeed, there usually is also a more or less hid-

Selected mental models and corresponding constellation formats

den advantage in not solving the problem. Whenever this becomes apparent, it is possible to see what has hitherto made it difficult to approach the problem. Finally one has to acknowledge that each objective is only a step on the way to completing a greater task. Therefore it is useful to look also at the "subsequent step" so that the problem is placed in an enlarged framework.

Here an example makes clear what has just been written. A management team established that customer complaints about the efficiency of the maintenance service had increased drastically. The quality of maintenance had always been an important selling point. A workshop with the managers of the maintenance service, sales, production and the managing director produced no positive result. Many possible causes were listed, but they could not agree on the measures to be taken. Ultimately, the consultant suggested doing a system constellation.

There was quick agreement on the objective of continuing to guarantee the specified service level. The first ambiguities appeared when assigning responsibilities: "Who is responsible for this objective: the service department? Sales? The managing director?" In the end the managing director took responsibility for the topic. The obstacles listed were:

- The increased complexity of equipment after the addition of two new product lines,
- the growing impatience of consumers who are under pressure by new government regulations,
- overworked employees,
- the communication difficulties between the maintenance and sales departments.

The following resources should help to achieve the objective:

- a sufficient number of maintenance technicians,
- the expertise of sales staff,
- support of the service hotline.

The "hidden advantage" of the problem was for a start not otherwise specified. The managers also had no clear picture of the "subsequent step".

Each of elements was noted on a sheet of paper and the managers were asked to place the sheets on the floor in order to make the structure of the problem visible. Afterwards the managers took up the position to which they felt attracted.

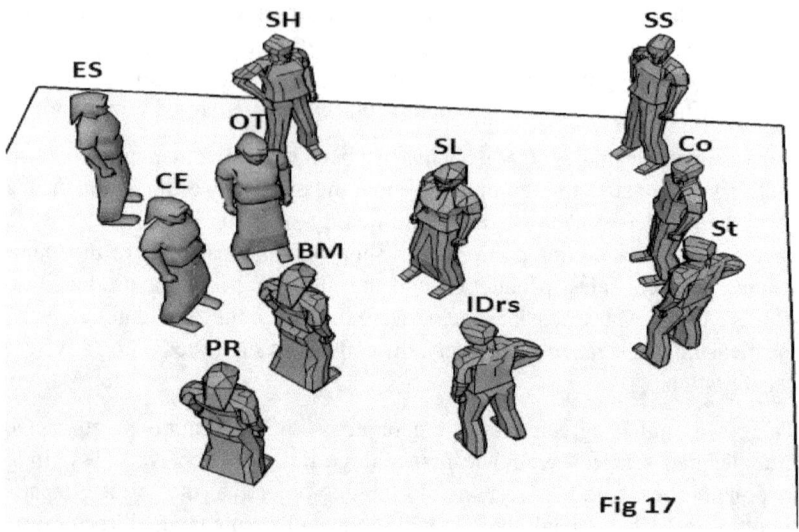

Fig. 17: Problematic situation - initial image

The lack of order of the initial situation (Fig. 17) reflects clearly the confusion of the preceding discussion. Several of the dysfunctional elements were however immediately recognizable:
- the management was focussed solely on the service level,
- they were irritated by the *overwork of the service department*, but did not want to pay any attention to it,
- the *hidden advantage* or, in other words the *price to pay* for the solution turned out to be "the policy of not employing extra staff" that had been decided as the answer to the financial crisis.

The constellation process, lasting more than 70 minutes, was interrupted several times in order to interpret the movements of the representatives and transform them into precise measures. The representatives only began to relax when *management* moved near to the *price* - an expression of the awareness that a solution was not possible without an appropriate price. The constellation only came to an end once all elements had found a good place (fig. 18).

Selected mental models and corresponding constellation formats 123

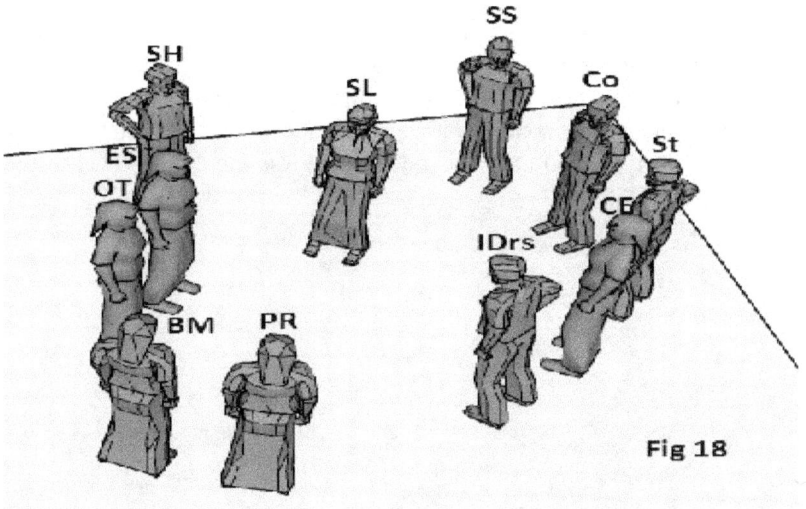

Fig. 18: *Problematic situation - final image*

SM Senior management (focus)
ES extra staff (Resource)
SL Service Level (objective)
St staff support (Resource)
CE Complexity of equipment (obstacle)
SH Service Hotline (Resource)

IDr Impatience of Drs. (obstacle)
PR Price
OE Overwork of employees (obstacle)
SS subsequent step
Co Communication (obstacle)

Consequently the stop in recruitment was challenged and the pressure of work on the employees was recognized. They thought about whether other departments might have extra personnel they could spare. In addition, they entertained the idea of including part of the maintenance costs in the customer's service contract. They recognized that the communication difficulties between the maintenance service and sales was attributable above all to the pressure of work on the technicians and commissioned the sales manager and the manager of the maintenance service to work out measures to support the sales staff and improve communication with the consumers. The increased complexity of the product range should be seen more from the point of view of the competitive advantages and not from the maintenance problems. The "subsequent step" can be interpreted as follows: if we extend our range of products as planned, then we have to provide for the appropriate maintenance service from the outset.

6.3.3 Resolving conflicts

A multitude of models describes the origin and resolution of conflicts. Graph. 10 shows a model that focuses on what we consider to be the central conflicting factors and also on the wishes and fears, not openly expressed, that those concerned are often not aware of at all. The following constellation format illustrates how these factors can lead to the escalation of a conflict.

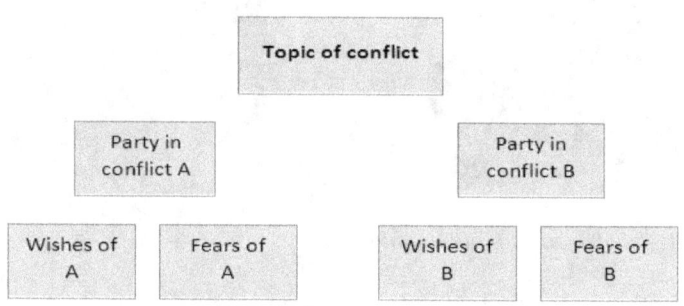

Graph. 10: Structuring a conflict

The constellation format is suitable both for discussions between two conflicting parties sitting at the same table as well as when only one party being present. Each party positions symbols or sheets of paper representing, wishes and fears on the table or on the floor. Dialogue and constellation can go hand in hand, i.e., each movement of the symbols is linked to the description of a change in behavior and conversely each statement can be transformed into a corresponding movement.

Selected mental models and corresponding constellation formats 125

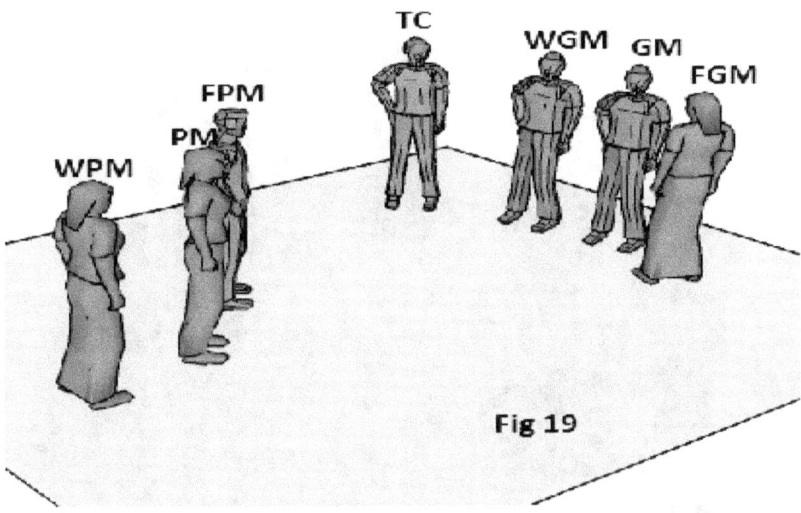

Fig. 19: Conflict dynamics - initial image

TC Topic of conflict: reducing costs
GM general manager
WGM Wishes of general manager:
precise measures

FGM Fears of GM
PM Production manager
WPM Wishes of PM
FPM Fears of PM: resistance of

The example of the conflict between a production manager and his boss the general manager illustrates the driving forces (fig. 19). The conflict revolves around the measures with which the company wants to react to a sales crisis. The general manager reproaches the production manager for not taking sufficiently strong measures to reduce costs. The production manager reproaches the GM saying that the latter thinks in the short-term and does not take on board the negative repercussions of his belt-tightening measures. The production manager feels that the GM's wish has put him under pressure, but has difficulties expressing what he really means. He cites especially his fear that the expected resistance of the workforce could have a negative effect on the savings measures. The GM has expressed his wishes, to implement immediate measures for cost savings. However, his behavior in the conflict situation is strongly influenced by fears that he has not mentioned. These divert his attention and make contact with the production manager more difficult.

126   *Enacting solutions*

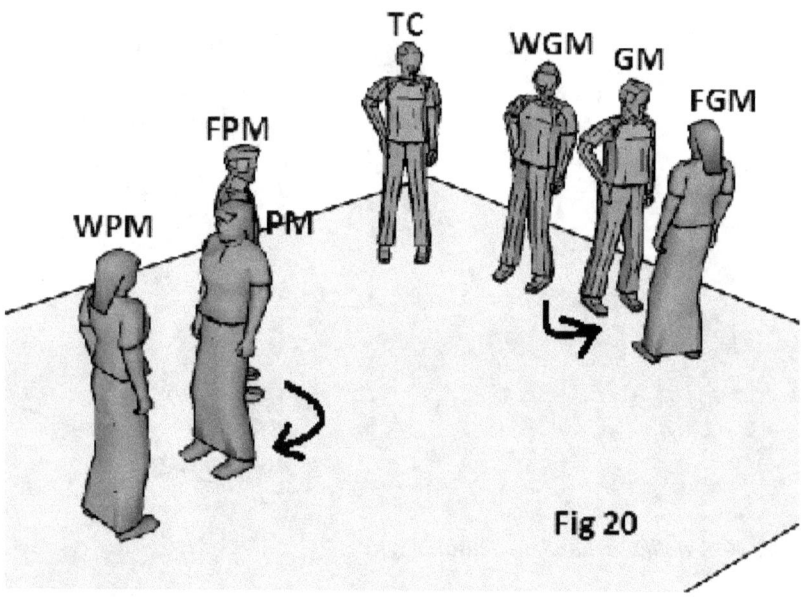

Fig. 20: Conflict Dynamics - provisional result

TC Topic of conflict   WGM Wishes of the GM: precise urgent measures
PM Production manager   FPM Fears of PM: resistance of workforce
GM General manager   FGM Fears of GM: Uncertainty about overcoming crisis
WPM Wishes of PM: participatory management style retained

The *production manager* is aware that he wants to retain his participatory management style and the positive working atmosphere. The GM doubts whether the measures he asked for are the right answer to the crisis. This clarification puts a positive spin on the discussions and in the end results in the constellation shown at fig. 21. The GM was able to express his doubts about the measures he had asked for. He now takes the *fears of the production manager* seriously. Both are looking for sustainable solutions together. The *production manager* can now give full rein to his *wish* for a participatory management style.

Selected mental models and corresponding constellation formats 127

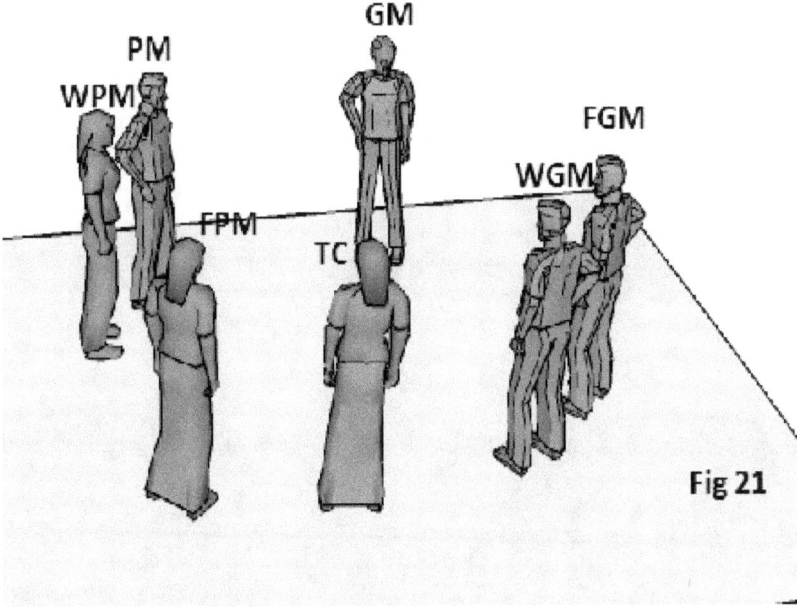

Fig. 21: *Conflict Dynamics - Solution*

TC Topic of conflict
GM General manager
WBM Wishes of GM

FBM Fears of GM
PM Production manager
WPM Wishes of PM
FPM Fears of PM

CHAPTER 7

COMPLEMENTARY METHODS AND TECHNIQUES

In a management context constellation work incorporates other methods from the domain of the learning organization. These methods use language because language is needed in order to focus on the specific interests of a team or group. Language is needed again in order to mutually understand the experience of a workshop so that a shared sense can be developed. On the one hand these methods prepare the field for a constellation by clarifying what has to be investigated and by specifying the system segment. On the other hand they serve to collectivize the results of the work and lead on to a renewed in-depth development of the topic or to the individual steps to a solution.

We explain and introduce at this point the most important methods used in connection with management constellations. Those are: Dialog according to David Bohm, World Café according to Juanita Brown, Open Space according to Harrison Owen, Dialogic Interview, Fish Bowl, the Recurring Question and the Four Rooms of Change.

7.1 Dialogue

According to David Bohm dialogue is a form of sharing each other's mind reciprocally. Holding individual opinion in suspense produces a common awareness that legitimizes and, at the same time, gives direction to the later action of individuals or the group. Bohm also speaks here of a collective sense. The dialogue turns individual awareness into a collective awareness. Dialogue therefore allows collective awareness to express itself.

In the dialogue setting the participants sit in a circle. At the beginning, a stone or some other object is placed in the centre and serves as a "silent" facilitator. Whoever picks up the stone can speak until he puts it back in the centre again or hands it to another participant. This procedure meets a very specific purpose. The discussion is slowed down so that the words gain more weight.

The dialogue is not so much about exchanging points of view but rather more about exploring common horizons. This is where dialogue differs from debate.

Dialogue promotes the following key competencies or attitudes:
- to take on the role of learner and not of an expert,
- to respect others,
- readiness to explain one's own way of thinking,
- concentrating on what is essential,
- compassionate listening,
- suspending one's own judgements and concentrating on facts and figures,
- productive pleading by disclosing assumptions and thinking processes instead of merely the outcomes of one's thoughts,
- to develop a questioning attitude,
- to observe the observers and notice how they react to each other.

Bohm tells us: "From time to time this group met together in their circle. They spoke and spoke apparently without reaching any obvious result. They took no decisions. There was no leader. Everyone could contribute to the discussion. Possibly more weight was given to the words of the wise men and women, the elders, but everyone was free to speak. The meeting went on until for no apparent reason it broke up and the group dispersed. But afterwards everybody seemed to know what had to be done because they all fitted into the big picture and because they all understood each other well. Then they were able to meet in small groups, do something and take decisions." (Bohm 1998)

We regularly insert a dialogue, carried out in accordance with dialogic principles, at the end of a constellation.

7.2 World Café

World Café is perhaps the most agreeable way to bring a large number of people, unknown to each other, together in an informal exchange of ideas that is nevertheless rich in content. This format of communication is based on the assumption that those interested already have enough knowledge, experience and creativity to cope with even the most difficult challenges.

At the same time, World Café facilitates the exploration of a specific topic *and* at the same time the concentration on relevant aspects. An in-depth, common knowledge for creative solutions can develop in the course of several rounds of discussions.

The idea of the World Café had its origins in the traditional 19th century coffee houses of Vienna and Paris, two of the world's most important cosmopolitan cities. Then the visitors to these places re-invented the world in animated discussions and mutually inspired each other.

In the World Café groups of four to six "guests" discuss a specific problem at small round or square tables, in a series of three (and sometimes more) discussions. These last 15 to 30 minutes and after each discussion all participants, except one, move to another table. The participant who remains behind briefly updates the new discussion panel about the most important insights of the preceding discussions. As a rule, these thoughts are picked up and developed further in the new discussions. New questions and ideas also surface.

By means of this "live network" the ideas expressed on the common subject relate to each other and gradually build up to the first approaches of a solution. At the end of the discussions, the various aspects are brought together and visualized. The result can be the starting point for a further development in a management constellation.

The etiquette of a World Café is:
- concentrate on what is happening.
- let others participate in your experience.
- speak about what is affecting you at the moment.
- try to really understand the other person.
- gather ideas and link them into a larger whole.
- listen for shades of meaning.
- draw, doodle and write on paper serviettes.

As a rule, we use the World Café before the constellation in order to make the central topic clearer. An intermediate step however is still needed to clarify the matter precisely.

7.3 Open Space

Open Space is the most basic of all the large-group interventions. The predetermined structural elements are, in addition to a central problem, just the plenum and a number of workshops that run parallel. The latter have a fixed time period of 45 to 90 minutes.

The participants introduce those aspects that interest them and in which they want to immerse themselves with like-minded people in the Open Space.

The Open Space format builds on the self-organising powers in groups. Accordingly the interventions are reduced to a minimum. Essentially they concentrate on:

- defining the topic,
- explaining the procedures and rules of the game and
- observing the times of the exchange of view in the plenum.

Harrison Owen, the inventor of Open Space, was inspired by the animated discussions in the intervals of conferences as well as by the dialogic art of discussion in tribal societies.

The following basic rules are valid:

- whoever is in the group is exactly the right person.
- whatever happens, it is the only thing that can happen.
- whenever it begins, it is the right time.
- whenever it is finished, it is finished. And when it is not finished, it is not finished.

Once a facilitator has introduced the topic and the rules of the Open Space, the participants write one or several inspiring topics on a sheet of A4 paper. These topics are briefly outlined to the group. Afterwards they stick the sheets of paper with their topics on a board showing a grid of workrooms and working hours ("Agenda"). The next step is for all participants to register for the workshops dealing with the topics that interest them.

The topics are discussed in the workshops and first solutions are developed. The results of the workshops are put down on paper and made available to all participants.

The participants of an Open Space session are free to leave an ongoing workshop or if they prefer to join another one already underway (known as "bumble-bee") or also to skip workshops to go for a walk, think about things or to talk with some like-minded participants (known as "butterflies").

We adopt the Open Space in large groups at the end of constellation work. The individual aspects that have become visible during the constellation can easily be picked up and furthered.

7.4 Dialogic Interview

This form of discussion is shaped by interested exploration. Together with a single interlocutor or with the team members or with a small group the facilitator sounds out the topic put forward. Openness is crucial for what has to be expressed. The facilitator makes sure that attention is directed gradually more to the differences that could produce a good solution for the people and groups involved. During the discussion he notes the points that seem important to him on a flip chart. These are reference points for the discovery of the elements of a constellation.

7.5 Fish Bowl

In the case of the fish bowl method a small group of participants discuss a specific topic in the inner circle of a larger plenum while the other participants listen to the discussion in an outer circle without taking part directly in the proceedings. If a participant in the outer circle would like to make a contribution to the discussion then he can sit down in an empty chair in the inner circle. He gives up this chair again once he has made his point. The facilitator sits in the inner circle and guides the discussion with his questions. It is helpful if a participant or a second facilitator can note the results of the discussion on a flip chart.

The fish bowl technique is very well suited for use in a medium-sized group for clarifying the matter and determining the elements.

7.6 The recurring question

The technique of the recurring question is also used before a constellation. The workshop participants sit in pairs opposite each other and keep asking the same question. With the help of these questions they gradually make contact with their perception of a specific topic. The participant who asks the question listens attentively to the answer without making any comment. He can repeat the question several times, but he should take care not to interrupt the chain of thought of the other person. After about ten minutes it is changed.

Now the participant, who has previously given his thoughts free rein, asks his colleague precisely the same question. It is possible to change several times. Subsequently, individual findings are shared in a discussion managed in accordance with the dialogue principles (cf. section 7.1). An issue for the group as a whole is identified and the elements for the constellation are determined.

7.7 Four rooms of change

Claes Janssen developed his theory of the "Four Rooms of Change" (Janssen 1996) on the basis of an elementary distinction. We can take up two positions in the event of a change.

For example, one would be to say "No" and reject the change; the other would be to say "Yes" and accept the change. Both alternatives can be favoured from either a positive or a negative mind-set. By combining positions and mind sets we obtain the following matrix (see table 4).

NO +	YES +
I am happy and see no reason to change anything	I have discovered a new way and make progress with the renewal.
NO −	YES −
I refuse to see the reasons for a change and hold on tightly to what is long-established.	I agree with the change, but I am confused and unsure.

Table 4: Matrix of mental attitudes

Janssen has written on his homepage (www.claesjanssen.com): "In all change, we move from a Contentment, which is lost, via a period in Denial, which is a defence of the old, through Confusion, which ends when we give up whatever it is of the old that had to be given up. The giving up is the turning point, making us open to the possibilities, the new, whereby we move on to Renewal."

Janssen also calls his model the "Four Rooms Apartment". The metaphor of the rooms describes impressively how we experience the world in the respective phase. The walls limit our view of the world where the satisfied colleague does not understand those who are confused and whoever is in the room of refusal cannot relate to those who are advancing the change.

If we follow the metaphor of the rooms, the doors that join the rooms have a significant importance. How do we move from confusion to renewal? How can we leave the room of confusion in order to advance via the unavoidable phase of confusion to new possibilities? The doors extend the model by a further four parameters (Graph. 11).

A peculiarity of the room of denial and resistance is that we also refuse to see that we are trapped in it. We feign satisfaction for ourselves and others and adhere firmly to our old models. To give them up would mean forfeiting part of our identity. "Acknowledge what is" is written on the door that leads us from the room of rejection into the room of uncertainty and confusion. "Let go of what has passed" opens the door to the room of renewal. "Creative compromise" opens the door to the room of satisfaction. So that we do not feel that we have to stay there forever, there is a door with the inscription "That's OK, it is enough". Many people find precisely this last inscription difficult.

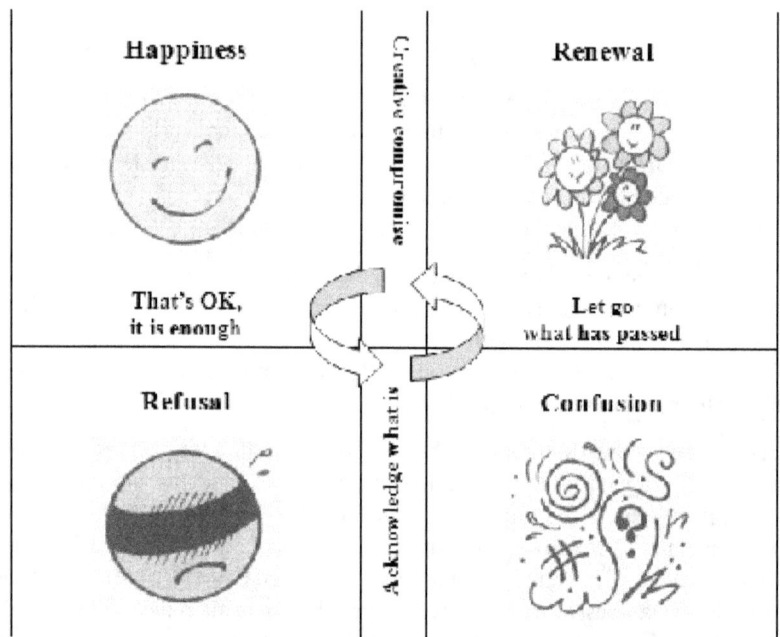

Graph. 11: Model of the four rooms of change

One of the most valuable qualities of the model is that it can create consensus. Janssen quotes R. D. Laing on his homepage: "If we cannot produce unity, the only honest beginning and perhaps also the only possible end of the meeting is that we agree to disagree." The model of the four rooms for change allows each member of a team to take up a position without having to expose himself to the judgement of the others. The four rooms are equivalents; each represents a necessary phase of the change.

In order to collectivise the findings of a constellation, we sometimes mark out the four fields of the model on the floor and invite the managers to take up a position in that field that corresponds to their current attitude and to express their thoughts from this position.

The managers can also simply be asked to write their thoughts on pieces of paper and place them in the corresponding field. The barriers to understanding vanish. Everyone can see from which room his colleague is speaking and can link his message to the respective context and understand it better. Often someone in the "yes" room is confronted by someone in the "no" room with his own shadow. This explains why they oppose each other so fiercely and at the same time get along so well.

We also invite managers to go into another field in order to experience "from inside" what they have seen "outside". As a result they frequently say: "Now at last I can understand what your mean!" It is clear to the team members that each statement is coupled to a specific spatial and temporal perspective that can change in another phase.

In this way the "Four rooms of change" model helps us to comprehend the dynamic aspect and complexity of information that have appeared in the constellation:
• part of the finding (YES+) is immediately clear and can be acted on immediately.
• possibly new questions have arisen in the constellation (YES–), to which an answer has to be found.
• resistance (NO–) can also create value by reducing the speed of change to a justifiable degree.
• ultimately what should be conserved (YES+) is highly valued because it represents an important aspect of identity.

Precisely recognizing resistance and refusal is often difficult and it is not always easy to face up to the confusion and uncertainty. It is no surprise that managers are constantly assessed on their ability to have the right solution to a problem immediately ready. In this way the model of the "Four rooms of change" creates a certain relief because it gives "permission" to show scepticism, restraint and refusal.

This model has proven itself also in the individual setting for finding the elements for a constellation and processing the findings of that constellation. It helps the client to clarify what can be implemented immediately, what needs more time to mature and what can remain as it is.

CHAPTER 8

CONSTELLATION WORK AS SENSEMAKING

In the meantime hardly anyone can seriously doubt that system constellations have their effect. On the other hand, there is disagreement about what constellations really are and many attempts have been made to find an answer or explanation. Are they a modern oracle, as Michael Zirkler somewhat provocatively floated during his contribution at a convention? Are they a form of trans verbal language as Matthias Varga von Kibéd describes them? Are they the movement of the soul as now seen by Bert Hellinger? Or are they quite simply occasions for telling stories with a sad beginning and a happy end?

It is often asserted that system constellations expose the truth. On this note Jakob Schneider records (Schneider 2008, p. 17): "Constellations deal with truth." He adds directly that such a statement is not without risk. Immediately before, he links the concept of truth to that of love, strength, order and spirit. And so one could impute to him that he sees a practice in system constellations that is in service to what is true, good and beautiful. With this he has classified himself and many other consultants in a tradition of thought that has its origins in German idealism.

We now suggest a somewhat different conceptualization of constellation work orientated towards American pragmatism. Indeed, we do not dispute that the system constellation shows a very specific form of perception and with it knowledge to the best advantage. However, we maintain that it is a matter of "sensemaking", i.e., making sense of something, and not a manifestation of a higher mental order.

Usually we resort to the system constellation, especially in working contexts, if we have not found another way out of a troublesome situation.

In the course of the constellation process what Claus Otto Scharmer (Scharmer 2000) paraphrases in his Theory U takes place: "to sense, enact and embody the future as it emerges." i.e., the development of the future. This future does not consist of a repetition of what is already well-known. It is something new and liberating. It allows us to explain the moment of relief that at the same time signifies the end of a constellation. The client is no longer trapped in a series of constricting practices. He has abandoned the burden of the past and feels free to do what is available *at the moment*.

As we understand it, constellation work has a solution in sight that is easy to act upon and aims to release energy for a first move towards this solution. In this regard to operate with the concept of truth seems rash to us. Because a picture of the future and the impulse to realize this cannot be described as "true" or "false" but probably as "plausible" in terms of coherent and conclusive matter. This plausibility is precisely a central aspect of the "sensemaking" processes.

"Sensemaking" is always stimulated whenever things appear in our experience that attract our attention and that we cannot immediately label and integrate into our current knowledge. We register them in our mind as irritating data. Speaking about this however produces ambiguity that in turn causes unease or anxiety. The data simply do not (yet) make sense. In addition, *coordinated action* is blocked and that is of special importance in an organizational context. That only changes with the next move. With the help of iterative search processes, the ambiguity can be reduced. What is eventually understood comes partly from the explanatory notes that have stood the test of time and partly from the intensive irritation caused by the available data.

Whether a specific interpretation then becomes part of existing knowledge and is thus available for other cases, depends on whether it is compatible with this pre-existing knowledge. If the interpretation complements existing knowledge, it is used to extend this. If it contradicts it, it is then simply forgotten again.

Karl E. Weick, to whose thoughts these statements can be traced back, has called the elements of the sensemaking "enactment", "selection" and "retention" and presented them together as in diagram 12 and related them to the stream of experience that he described in his model as the "ecological environment".

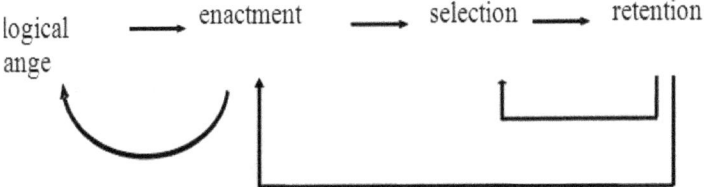

Graph. 12: Elements of sensemaking

The concept of **ecological change** stands for those changes that attract attention and even initiate a sensemaking process. They are the basic material for "sensemaking". As long as everything runs as usual, there is no cause for sensemaking.

Enactment is the directly cognitive and operational interaction of the protagonists with their environment. On the one hand the protagonists react to changes by extracting specific aspects out of context and trying to give them a name. On the other hand, they themselves provoke changes in turn by their (re-)actions. Ambiguous "coarse talk" is a product of enactment and it is imperative to transform this into coherent explanations.

This is done by **selection** i.e., by "imposing" rules and structures. These take the shape of causal maps – "mind maps". They include variables whose relevance is ensured by earlier experience.

Retention means storing the results of the selection. These are those causal maps that confer conclusiveness to the phenomena observed. Karl E. Weick calls them "designed environments".

The four elements interact with each other. Knowledge stored in retention impacts on interpretation as well as on the perception of "our" world. Enactment, for its part, influences selection and possibly causes us to modify our mind maps.

According to Weick, "sensemaking" has the following features:
• it is a continuous process without a beginning or an end.
• it creates the identity of a system and is itself based on this identity at the same time.
• a number of people are always involved in the process. They exchange views with each other in communities of practice.
• furthermore "sensemaking" is geared to action and not just to ideas.

- it refers to perceived phenomena taken incidentally from a wide abundance; Weick speaks of extracted cues.
- "Sensemaking" also takes place with an eye on what has gone before and retrospectively on remembered experience of life.
- and, as already mentioned, it is based on plausibility and not on accuracy or even truth.

Example of use

The following example offers an illustration of what has already been written.

In the margins of a meeting two area managers are comparing notes about a decline in sales that appears not to be due to cyclical fluctuations. At this particular time, they are not attaching too much significance to this. Apparently their colleagues did not face such a reduction in sales and so it was not mentioned in the meeting.

But that changed in the following discussion. The turnover statistics showed reductions across the board. No plausible explanation could be found for this. The economic situation was stable and they considered themselves to be market leaders "on the safe side". In the long run what counts is the quality of products. Had their customers not yet absorbed the last increase in prices? Had they overlooked important innovations of competitors at the last trade fair?

Somehow no answers could be found to this phenomenon. Some managers had heard from their sales personnel that long-standing customers were delaying their decision to buy. What could be the reason for this? To begin with the managers were at a loss.

Up to the present time the strategy of the product leadership had always borne fruit! This is how the reduction in sales became a top priority. Customers were systematically asked and a picture that made sense slowly evolved from single pieces of the jigsaw. A slick competitor had obviously succeeded in acquiring the customers by innovative auxiliary services. It is in fact logical that something like this could have prospects for success as every crafty marketing fox knows! Now they were again "master of the situation" and could consider arrangements for putting things right.

Admittedly this brief story is very usual. But it demonstrates very clearly that the "crisis" comes very quietly and many do not notice it coming. After things have returned to normal again, everyone is much wiser. However, until things are back to normal again, one or the other entanglement has to be resolved.

Weick's organizational concept

For constellation work in management contexts, we think it is helpful and useful to follow Weick's explanations for a little longer still. In his basic work "The Social Psychology of Organizing" (Weick 1995a) Weick convincingly states that *organization has its origins in sensemaking processes*. For this reason, he takes up a different position to traditional business economics that so far has looked on organizations as instruments for reaching an intended purpose: "Organizations are regarded as inventions of man, inventions that are imposed on the flow of life and force a certain order on it for a moment." For Weick organizing is a collective process of sensemaking. And he anticipates an essential aspect of systemic organizational theory. He focuses radically on the enactment or rather on the process of organizing.

Such a designation may appear strange at first glance, because organizations seem to consist of something made of people or buildings, long corridors or piles of files or all of them together.

In fact however, organizations do not change whenever for example employees pursue their own activities after a change of shift and other employees take their place. Organizations are also not the sum total of their employees. They are indeed dependent on people. Employees are a resource. But organizations themselves are merely the way people relate to each other in order to make sense together.

Buildings, assets and piles of paper are on the other hand quasi only "secondary effects" of the organization. That is what emerges if decisions made in organizations are more or less coordinated and decision making is always framed for its part in the processes of sensemaking.

Consequently, it is essential to move away from the idea that organizations are something substantial. A grand building on a well-known lakeside promenade is indeed the "feudal" representation of an organization. But the organization itself is not this grand building. It consists "only" of a series of fleeting events more or less correlated through the creation of sense and meaning and that can eventually lead to the construction of grand buildings. Here is Karl Weick once again: "Most 'things' in organizations are really relationships, variables linked together in a systematic way".

Constellation work as a process of collective sensemaking

After this trip into Karl E. Weick's world of thought and ideas, we now want to return to constellation work. We take the model of sensemaking because from our point of view it is eminently suitable for constellation work and the accompanying communication processes. We even maintain:

On a structural level there is a close similarity between organizing, producing sense and making a constellation.

We can also discern the following **four elements** in the case of constellation work according to the process of sensemaking (Graph. 13):

1. Clients expose their "inner image" of a problem to the spotlight. They create a dynamic context that could also, according to Weick, be seen as a stream of experience with which as a consequence they interact. Therefore it makes a lot of sense to describe constellations as simulations. Usually in problematic situations we face questions that cannot be answered. Heinz von Foerster defines these as follows (von Foerster and Pörksen 1998, p. 157): "In the case of questions that cannot in principle be answered we have shaken off every form of restraint, even that of logic, and with the freedom gained have also assumed responsibility for reaching decisions. We are all free to decide who we want to be and with this decision we also assume responsibility to decide about our existence." Constellation topics are also often questions to situations that appear to be hopeless. These difficulties can simply not be tackled with the current formulae.

2. At first, the dynamics the representatives express and that are inherent in the represented situation irritate (enactment). Everyone focuses full attention on what is happening. The representatives produce, as Weick would describe it, ambiguous "coarse talk" by conveying their body resonance. This meets the facts presented and at the same time points beyond them. Certain new aspects that appear can be discussed later. Aspects that have been overlooked can be included in the process of sensemaking. On the other hand, what is unnecessary can be excluded. New relevancies emerge. The gradual feeling of relief and comments regarding the perceived differences after a repositioning of the representatives indicate a compatible solution.

3. The clients interpret what surfaces in the constellation (selection). How they do this is always strongly shaped by their know-how. In this phase the changeover in the management constellation from the scenic to the linguistic medium takes place (Rosselet and Pedrocchi 2006, p. 73). We recommend that this changeover is implemented explicitly, clearly and precisely.

If we do not clearly separate perception from reflection, then the weak signals that can be captured via the body resonance are ignored. There is a risk that an explanation or a logical structure, fed from the world of thought, is hastily "imposed" and indeed not only by the clients but also by the facilitator. The acceptance of not knowing seems very important at this point.

4. In a dialogue clients gradually agree on a sensible interpretation (retention). This interpretation partly confirms existing knowledge and partly challenges it. In other words, learning takes place. As Andrea Berreth (Berreth 2009) has shown, learning in a management team is more likely to begin with adaptive single-loop-learning than innovative double-loop-learning. As we suspect the course for single or double-loop-learning is set not only during the actual constellation work but also in the sequence before it (cf. section 5.3). It depends on the topic and corresponding system segment on which the work is focused whether the constellation is used in order to investigate the alternatives of a decision process (e.g., "Do we have the same objective as our potential alliance partners?") or in order to reflect critically on the premises for reaching a decision (e.g., "Is the way we deal with the foot-dragging of the strategic alliance partner promising or not?"). In the first case it presumably amounts to single-loop-learning and in the second case to double-loop-learning.

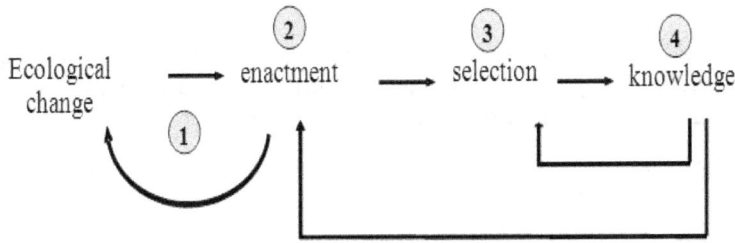

Graph. 13: structural similarity of "sensemaking" and constellation work

Against this theoretical background it is once again clear what matters in management constellations:

• the problem of a group or team is in the centre *relating to the success of the company as a whole or a division of a company* and not to the destiny of a single person or rather the cooperation between the members of a group.

- the focus rests on the *patterns of variables that account for the collective mental models and routines*, and not on the entanglements between individuals.

- it is a matter of *visualizing the first moves towards a compatible solution* and not about placing the elements in the "right order" . The *viability – i.e., the usefulness – of solutions* is important to us and not truth and accuracy.

- the *collective experience from irritation to information* is the central moment of constellation work and not the catharsis experienced by the main protagonist during a sort of rite of passage. We radically understand the constellation work as a process of collective sensemaking.

- the management constellation is always *embedded in the dialogic methods compatible with the concept of learning organization*. The latter offers support at a linguistic level when trying to make sense together.

- the *modelling of the relevant system segment for processing the problem* gains a central significance. We use different formats for this. Management models as heuristic patterns have always proven to be helpful and useful.

We should like to close this section on future prospects by quoting from Karl E. Weick's "The Social Psychology of Organizing. It might be that the invitation attached to it could provoke a sensemaking process. But that need not be the case.

"Organizations keep people busy, sometimes entertain them, impart a variety of experience, keep them away from the streets, offer excuses for telling stories and facilitate socialization. They have nothing else to offer."

What would happen if the word "organization" were to be replaced by the word "constellation"?

Selected Bibliography

Argyris, Chr. a. D. Schön (1978): *Organizational Learning: A Theory of Action Perspective* (Addison-Wesley)

Baecker, D. (1999): *Organization als System.* Frankfurt (Suhrkamp).

Baecker, D. (2003): *Organization und Management.* Frankfurt (Suhrkamp).

Bandler, R. (1985): *Using Your Brain--For a Change*: Neuro-Linguistic Programming (Real People Press).

Bateson, G. (2000): *Steps to an Ecology of Mind: Collected Essays in Anthropology, Psychiatry, Evolution, and Epistemology* (University of Chicago Press).

Berreth, A. (2007): *Innovation im Change-Management – Ist Innovation machbar? oder Die Übersetzungsleistung des Managements.* Basel (WWZ).

Berreth, A. (2009): *Organizationsaufstellung und Management.* Lesarten einer beraterischen Praxis. Heidelberg (Carl-Auer).

Boar, B. (2001): *The Art of Strategic Planning for Information Technology.* New York City (John Wiley & Sons).

Bohm, D. (1996): *On Dialog.* London (Routledge).

Bohnsack, Ralf (1999): *Rekonstruktive Sozialforschung.* Opladen (Leske + Budrich), 3. Aufl . 2003.

Buzan, T. e B. (2008): *The Mind Map Book: Unlock Your Creativity, Boost Your Memory, Change Your LifeBrown* (BBC Books).

J. u. D. Isaacs (2005): *The World Cafe: Shaping Our Futures Through Conversations That Matter.* San Francisco (Berrett Koehler).

Bude, H. (1985): *Der Sozialforscher als Narrationsanimateur.* Kölner Zeitschrift für Soziologie und Sozialpsychologie (37): 327–336.

Cohn, R. (1975): *Von der Psychoanalyse zur Themenzentrierten Interaktion.* Stuttgart (Klett-Cotta).

Essen, S. (2003): *Autopoietische Aufstellungsarbeit.* Praxis der Systemaufstellung (6) 2, 34–39.

Foerster, H. von u. B. Pörksen (1998): *Wahrheit ist die Erfindung eines Lügners.* Heidelberg (Carl-Auer).

Forrester, J. (1968): *Principles of Systems* (Pegasus Communications).

Foucault, M. (1966): *Les mots et les choses. Paris* (Gallimard).

Giddens, A. (1984): *The Constitution of Society: Outline of the Theory of Structuration.* Berkeley (University of California Press).

Goldberg, P. (1985): *The Intuitive Edge: Understanding and Developing Intuition.* Los Angeles (Tarcher).

Goleman, D. (1996): *Emotional Intelligence* (Bantam Books).

Grochowiak, K. u. J. Castella (2001): *Systemdynamische Organizationsberatung.* Heidelberg (Carl-Auer).

Groth, Th. (2004): *Organizationsaufstellungen in Theorie und Praxis.* Vortrag auf der Arbeitstagung d. Intern. Forums für Systemaufstellungen in Arbeitskontexten und Organizationen (infosyon) e. V.

Groth, Th. u. G. Stey (Hrsg.) (2007): *Potentiale der Organizationsaufstellung.* Innovative Ideen und Anwendungsbereiche. Heidelberg (Carl-Auer).

Hartkemeyer, M., J. F. Hartkemeyer u. L. Freeman Dhority (1998): *Miteinander denken. Das Geheimnis des Dialogs.* Stuttgart (Klett-Cotta).

Hellinger, B. (1996): *Love's Hidden Symmetry: What Makes Love Work in Relationships* (Zeig, Tucker & Theisen).

Isaacs, W. (1999): *Dialogue and the art of thinking together.* New York (Doubleday/Random House).

James, J. (1997): *Thinking in Future Tense: Leadership Skills for a New Age.* Glencoe, Illinois (Free Press).

Janssen, Cl. (1996): *The four rooms of change – Förändringens fyra rum.* Stockholm (Wahlström & Widstrand).

Jong, P. de u. I. Kim Berg (1998): *Interviewing for Solutions.*

Kaplan, R. S. u. Norton D. P. (2004): *Strategy Maps: Converting Intangible Assets into Tangible Outcomes*

Königswieser, R. u. A. Exner (1998): *Systemische Interventionen.* Stuttgart (Klett-Cotta), 5. Aufl. 2000.

Luhmann, N. (1990): *Theory of Society* (Stanford University Press).

Magee, P. (1996): *Brain dancing.* Bordentown, NJ (Magee Research).

Mandl, Chr. (2006): *Gewissheit, Risiko und Neues.* In: Chr. Mandl u. K. Sohn

(Hrsg.): Aufgabe Zukunft: Versäumen, planen, ermöglichen. Zürich (Versus).

Nagel, R. u. R. Wimmer (2002): *Systemische Strategieentwicklung.* Stuttgart (Klett-Cotta).

Neuweg, G. H. (1999): *Könnerschaft und implizites Wissen.* Münster (Waxmann), 3. Aufl. 2004.

Nonaka, I. u. H. Takeuchi (1997): *The knowledge-creating company* (Oxford University Press).

Norman, R., Ramirez, R. (1998): *Designing Interactive Strategy.* Hoboken, NJ (Wiley).

O'Connor, J.; McDermott, I. (1997): *The art of systems thinking.* London (Thorsons).

Owen, H. (1997): *Open space technology. A Users Guide.* San Francisco (Berrett-Koehler).

Pedrocchi, L. u. C. Rosselet (2007): *Management Constellations.* In: Th. Groth u. G. Stey (Hrsg.): *Das Potential der Organizationsaufstellung.* Heidelberg (Carl-Auer).

Polanyi, M. (1966): *The Tacit Dimension.* Chicago (University of Chicago Press).

Porter, M. (1998): *Competitive Advantage: Creating and Sustaining Superior Performance* (Free Press)

Probst, G., St. Raub u. K. Romhardt (1997): *Wissen managen.* Wiesbaden (Gabler), 4. Aufl . 2003.

Rosselet, C. (2003): *Mit der Organizationsaufstellung die Firma durchleuchten.* io new management (72) 12: 47–51.

Rosselet, C. (2005): *Von der Irritation zur Information – Systemaufstellung und Managementpraxis.* OrganizationsEntwicklung 3: 16–27.

Rosselet, C. u. L. Pedrocchi (2006): *Die Systemaufstellung für Management-Kontexte neu formatiert.* Praxis der Systemaufstellung (9) 2: 73–81.

Rosselet, C., G. Senoner u. H. K. Lingg (2007): *Management Constellations – Mit der Systemaufstellung Komplexität managen.* Stuttgart (Klett-Cotta).

Rüegg-Stürm, J. (2002): *Das neue St. Galler Management-Modell.* Bern (Haupt).

Schein, E. H. (1998): *Process Consultation Revisited: Building the Helping*

Relationship. (Prentice Hall)

Scharmer, C. O. (2000): *Presencing: Learning from the future as it emerges.* Lecture presented at the Conference on Knowledge and Innovation, Helsinki School of Economics.

Scharmer, C. O. (2008): *Theory U. Leading from the future as it emerges.* San Francisco (Berrett-Koehler).

Schlötter, P. (2005): *Vertraute Sprache und ihre Entdeckung.* Heidelberg (Carl-Auer).

Schmid, B. (1994): *Wo ist der Wind, wenn er nicht weht?* Paderborn (Junfermann).

Schneider, J. (2007) *Systemaufstellung und Quantenphysik.* Praxis der Systemaufstellung (10) 2: 18–20.

Schneider, J. (2008): *Wie wirken Systemaufstellungen?* Praxis der Systemaufstellung (11) 1: 17–25.

Schreyögg, G. u. Ch. Noss (1995): *Organisatorischer Wandel: Von der Organizationsentwicklung zur lernenden Organization.* Betriebswirtschaft 55 (2): 169–185.

Schumacher, Th. (2000): *Systemische Strukturen in Familie und Organizationen. Eine Studie von Auswirkungen auf Familienaufstellungen auf subjektive Beziehungsbilder.* Bonn (Rheintal).

Schulz von Thun, F. (1981): *Miteinander reden: Stoerungen und Klaerungen: Psychologie der zwischenmenschlichen Kommunikation* (Rowohlt Tb.).

Senge, P. (1999): *The dance of change.* New York (Crown Business).

Senoner, G. (2006): *Verstehen, Entscheiden, Führen und Beraten.* In: W. De Philipp (Hrsg.): *Systemaufstellung im Einzelsetting.* Heidelberg (CarlAuer).

Shazer, St. de (1985): *Keys to Solution in Brief Therapy* (W W Norton).

Sheldrake, R. (1988): *The Presence of the Past: morphic resonance and the habits of nature* (Times Books).

Senge, P. M. (1990): *The fifth discipline.* New York (Doubleday/Currency).

Simon, F. B. (2004): *Gemeinsam sind wir blöd!? Die Intelligenz von Unternehmen, Managern und Märkten.* Heidelberg (Carl-Auer).

Sparrer, I. u. M. Varga von Kibéd (1998): *Vom Familien-Stellen zur Systemischen Strukturaufstellungsarbeit.* In: G. Weber (Hrsg.): *Praxis des Familien-*

stellens. Beiträge zu systemischen Lösungen nach Bert Hellinger. Heidelberg (Carl-Auer), 3., überarb. Aufl. 2000.

Sparrer, I. (2001): *Wunder, Lösung und System*. Heidelberg (Carl-Auer).

Varga von Kibéd, M. u. I. Sparrer (2000): *Ganz im Gegenteil – für Querdenker und solche, die es werden wollen*. Heidelberg (Carl-Auer).

Von Bertalanffy, L. (2004): *General System Theory: Foundations, Development, Applications* (George Braziller).

Weber, G. (Hrsg.) (1993) *Zweierlei Glück. Das Familienstellen Bert Hellingers*. Heidelberg (Carl-Auer), 6. Aufl. 1995.

Weber, G. (Hrsg.) (1998): *Praxis des Familienstellens. Beiträge zu systemischen Lösungen nach Bert Hellinger*. Heidelberg (Carl-Auer), 3., überarb. Aufl. 2000.

Weber, G. u. B. Gross (1998): *Organizationsaufstellungen*. In: G. Weber (Hrsg.): *Praxis des Familienstellens. Beiträge zu systemischen Lösungen nach Bert Hellinger*. Heidelberg (Carl-Auer), 3., überarb. Aufl. 2000.

Weber, G. (Hrsg.) (2001): *Praxis der Organizationsaufstellungen. Grundlagen, Prinzipien, Anwendungsbereiche*. Heidelberg (Carl-Auer), 2., korr. Aufl. 2002.

Weber, G., G. Schmidt u. F. B. Simon (2005): *Aufstellungsarbeit revisited nach Bert Hellinger*. Heidelberg (Carl-Auer).

Weick, K. E. (1979a): *Social Psychology of Organizing* (Topics in Social Psychology) New York (Addison-Wesley).

Weick, K. E. (1995b): *Sensemaking in Organizations - Foundations for Organizational Science* (Sage).

Willke, H. (2004): *Einführung in das systemische Wissensmanagement*. Heidelberg (Carl-Auer).

Wimmer, R. (2003): *Die Steigerung der Lernfähigkeit von Organizationen*. In: M. Zirkler u. W. R. Müller (Hrsg.): *Die Kunst der Organizationsberatung*. Bern (Haupt).

Wittgenstein, L. (1971): *Philosophical Investigations* (Prentice Hall).

Wittgenstein, L. (1984): *Tractatus Logico-Philosophicus* (Kegan Paul).

The authors

Claude Rosselet, lic. Oec. HSG, founder of *Inscena Systemische Beratung GmbH* in Männedorf (Switzerland), coach and business consultant. Experience as manager in several companies; since 1994 consultant for executives and project teams as well as organizations in innovation and change processes; lecturer at several colleges and institutes; member of the editorial team of *Praxis der Systemaufstellungen,* founding member of *Infosyon - International Forum for System Constellations in Organizations.*

www.inscena.ch

Georg Senoner, MBA founder of SysMaCon – Systemic Management Consulting in Bolzano (Italy). Consultant and coach specializing in strategy and organization development. From 1975 – 1998 CEO of Sevi, an internationally operating toy company; Lecturer at Sistema Counseling (Milan); founding member of *Infosyon - International Forum for System Constellations in Organizations*

www.sysmacon.org

MANAGEMENT TOOLS

I - Lorenzo Cavalli, "Conoscenza e Gestione", 2008 - print + ebook (italian language)

II - Mauro Bozzola, "Progetti, Alleanze e Identità organizzative", 2008 - print (italian language)

III - Claude Rosselet e Georg Senoner, "Strutture del successo", 2011 - print + eBook (italian language)

IV - Claude Rosselet and Georg Senoner, "Enacting solution, 2013 - print + eBook (english language)

www.ingramcontent.com/pod-product-compliance
Lightning Source LLC
Chambersburg PA
CBHW051749230426
43670CB00012B/2217